The Sermon on the Mount

ITS LITERARY STRUCTURE
AND DIDACTIC PURPOSE

A Lecture delivered at Wellesley College May 20, 1901
and subsequently revised and enlarged with the
addition of Three Appendices
Adapted to exhibit by Analytical and Synthetic
Criticism the Nature and Interconnection
of the Greater Discourses of Jesus

BY

BENJAMIN W. BACON, D.D.

*Buckingham Professor of New Testament Criticism and
Exegesis in Yale University*

Wipf and Stock Publishers
EUGENE, OREGON

Wipf and Stock Publishers
199 West 8th Avenue, Suite 3
Eugene, Oregon 97401

The Sermon on the Mount
Its Literacy Structure and Didactic Purpose
By Bacon, Benjamin W.
ISBN: 1-59244-370-2
Publication date 10/1/2003
Previously published by The Macmillan Company, 1902

PREFACE

TEACHERS of biblical science are increasingly conscious of the need of a text-book of the higher criticism. This method is no longer an experiment. The New Testament, the Gospels above all, can be interpreted, as they have been in the past, without it; but the modern teacher who is ignorant on this score is justly considered incompetent. Baleful or beneficent, it must be understood.

Moreover, the discourses of Jesus furnish a problem that nothing else has solved and to which these methods must inevitably be applied. No scholar has ever attempted the construction of a gospel harmony without again and again being compelled to resort to expedients which do not represent the real meaning of his authorities. No student has ever penetrated beneath the surface of a "harmony" without dis-

covering again and again that the osten-
sible process is most inconsistently and
half-heartedly applied. In short, our four
authorities all differ in their form, order,
occasion, and connection of these sayings,
the most precious pearls of all literature.
What else can one do than compare and
test and try, sifting the evidence, reaching
back behind the reporters toward their
authorities, back to the original utterances
themselves? And the methods for so
doing must be approved and systematized.
To say this is to say that any impartial,
sincere effort to furnish an example of
these methods in application must be wel-
comed if prepared with reasonable qualification for the task.

Such is the purpose of the present volume. Its nucleus is simply a lecture prepared for delivery at Wellesley College,
Massachusetts, by the condensation of six
lectures previously delivered to the adult
Bible class of the United Church, New
Haven. Ultimate publication was promised on the first occasion to those who
asked opportunity to obtain them in print,

but the matter was delayed. At Wellesley similar requests followed the delivery of the lecture and were met by a renewal of the promise. In endeavoring to fulfil it the author has become convinced that this is the opportunity for meeting, so far as he is able, the larger need already spoken of. The lecture itself is printed substantially as delivered, though not without considerable additions, as well as footnotes. But from the nature of the case results could be presented by this means only in outline, in a simple, semi-popular way. Processes and evidences lay submerged. For the purposes of a text-book, however simple, it was needful to supplement this general exposition of the process and results by appendices devoted to an exhibition in somewhat greater detail of the methods and evidences. Accordingly, three appendices have been added to the lecture, the first mainly analytical, justifying the transpositions of material effected in the lecture to restore the original Discourse on the Higher Righteousness, by comparison of the two principal reporters,

Matthew and Luke.   The second appendix aims only to justify the choice of readings, as between authorities, for the material admitted as forming part of the Discourse. The third exemplifies the possibility of synthetic criticism in the restoration of some of the great discourses of Jesus, using nothing for the purpose outside the limits of the material wrongly connected by Matthew or Luke with the Discourse on the Higher Righteousness, as evidenced by the processes shown in Appendix I.

Completeness of treatment from this point of view would of course require much more.   At least the great parabolic discourses, particularly that of Mk. iv. and parallels, would have to be included, if not a discussion of the entire body of discourse material attributed to Jesus by the synoptic evangelists.   But this field is fortunately by no means neglected.   Wendt's *Lehre Jesu* has been followed by Jülicher's great work, *Die Gleichnissreden Jesu*, with ample discussion of the characteristic features of Jesus' teaching, and every treatise on New Testament theology has at least a chapter on the teaching of Jesus. Those of Weiss and Beyschlag are fortunately accessible to English readers, though Holtzmann has not yet found a translator. Professor George B. Stevens's recent treatise gives the English reader discussion at first hand. Our object is much more limited. Since it had necessarily become one of the main contentions of our address that the longer, connected discourses attributed to Jesus by our synoptic evangelists, of which the so-called Sermon on the Mount is the principal example, are not compositions of the evangelists, nor even in all cases the result of mere agglutination in the formative period of the gospels, it seemed well to supplement the principal example of a connected discourse, which certainly antedates our canonical gospels, by others which similarly might be regarded as examples of the *preaching* of Jesus as distinct from the mere apophthegms, parables, or sayings. A double purpose is subserved when the examples given embody the same material which our analysis reveals to have been mistakenly attached to the Discourse on the Higher Righteousness; for the synthesis will then corroborate the analysis. The appended notes will at least illustrate the nature of the problem which confronts the would-be biographer, as he endeavors by synthetic methods to ascertain the circumstances, occasion, and connection of these discourses.

Finally, it may do no harm to reiterate that fascinating as are the problems of source-analysis, particularly the conjectural restoration of the *Logia* (a problem distinct from the present, which goes quite behind the question of literary criticism regarding documentary sources, however primitive, to that of historical criticism, What did Jesus say?), the benefit of engaging in these studies is not merely, perhaps not mainly, in the direct ends achieved, but in the resultant acquirement of familiarity with the incomparable sayings of Jesus themselves, discriminating appreciation of their exact original sense, and historical understanding of their relation to his sublime career. Let all other results be null, and the insight attained in these ways by comparing *logion* with *logion*, report with report, will a thousandfold repay the effort; for no study of commentaries can compare with this method for elucidation of the real meaning.

Needless to say the application of such criticism involves no disrespect to our evangelists. That wherein Luke himself sets the example (Lk. i. 1–4) is not impious. That which meets our Lord's own teaching as to true searching of the Scriptures (Jn. v. 39–40; [R.V.] xvi. 13–14) would not give offence to those whose whole effort was to convey to us the story " even as delivered to them by those which from the beginning were eye-witnesses and ministers of the word," that we might "believe that Jesus is the Christ, the Son of God, and believing might have life through his name." If in other departments of biblical study the use of these methods may seem inevitably to involve the overthrow of traditional theories regarding the authorship of various writings and the infallible accuracy of the writers, here no such assumptions are permissible. No one claims that we have the sayings in the form or connection in which they were uttered. No one claims that here we have an original unit, which the pitiless critic aches to dissect. Here the disjecta membra are the original datum. Analysis can scarcely go further than a simple placing of the four gospels side by side already carries it, and as it was already acknowledged to be when Luke set himself the difficult task "to write them down in order." The work of the critic here is restoration. His method must be, if only for the sake of his science, to think himself to the utmost into the atmosphere and circumstances, yes, above all, into the spirit and ideals and feeling of Jesus of Nazareth. If there be prejudice among Christian people against the training of students in colleges and seminaries in such a method, we can await its disappearance with the patience which knows it cannot be long disappointed.

B. W. B.

New Haven,
December, 1901.

CONTENTS

PAGE

PREFACE v

LECTURE. THE DISCOURSE OF JESUS ON THE NEW LAW OF THE KINGDOM OF GOD CONSIDERED WITH REGARD TO ITS LITERARY STRUCTURE AND DIDACTIC PURPOSE 1

APPENDIX A. ANALYSIS OF THE DISCOURSE AS REPORTED BY OUR EVANGELISTS, WITH A VIEW TO ASCERTAINING THE ORIGINAL OCCASION AND CONTEXT OF THE ELEMENTS OF EXTRANEOUS ORIGIN 121

APPENDIX B. COMPARISON OF READINGS FOR RECONSTRUCTION OF THE DISCOURSE . . . 175

APPENDIX C. RECONSTRUCTION OF THE MORE IMPORTANT SYNAGOGUE DISCOURSES OF JESUS FROM WHICH ELEMENTS WOULD APPEAR TO HAVE BEEN ADDED BY OUR EVANGELISTS TO THE SERMON ON THE MOUNT 181

INDEX TO SCRIPTURE PASSAGES . . . 259

THE SERMON ON THE MOUNT

A STUDY IN SYNTHETIC CRITICISM OF THE GREATER DISCOURSES OF JESUS

I CONGRATULATE myself and my hearers on the subject whose selection we owe in part to others. The average thoughtful man, if asked to define the representative teaching of Jesus, will reply instinctively, "The Sermon on the Mount."

The Bible is Christo-centric, whether our theology be so or not. We may go further. Human thought and literature in its loftiest sphere, our relation to the unseen Source and Goal of all, are Christo-centric. An impartial historical estimate will admit that Jesus' life and teachings constitute the highest revelation of man to himself, and since "the invisible things of the creation are perceived through the things that are made," this revelation is also the highest of God to man. Thus in our ultimate questionings the light shed by him is "the light of the world."

So then, if there be anything in literature worth studying, it is his thought on these subjects; and "study" implies, in our day, the genetic method. We must appreciate Jesus in relation to his times; we must take what we know of him in the perspective of human thought and historical event, which leads up to him and down from him. And when it comes to actual, direct knowledge, we must come into touch with him by what he says himself, rather than by what any one says about him. Paul, the evangelists, are but "ministers through whom we believe"; their appreciation of him whom they knew so much better than we is our indispensable means of approach — but only a means. Never do they render us so great service as when they transmit to us unaltered, uncolored by application to the exigencies of their own situation, the remembered words of Jesus himself. Then we can say, with the men of Sychar, " Now we believe, not because of thy word, for we have heard him ourselves, and know that this is indeed the Saviour of the world."

And in turning thus to the most direct means of approach, it is natural, too, that men should not go to that gospel which is, by common consent of ancient and modern times, the latest in date, however well it may deserve in one sense the title, " heart of Christ." For in it, to an incomparably greater degree, the teachings of the Master are digested and assimilated to the evangelist's own thought. In John we find a selection of the doctrines of Jesus elaborated, adapted to meet the special erroneous tendencies of theosophic speculation at the end of the century in proconsular Asia. We must go rather to that which, by equally universal consent, emanates from the soil of Palestine, and, if not itself apostolic, at least embodies an indisputably

apostolic collection of Sayings of the Lord,
the *Logia*, as critics designate the work.
The vast majority of competent scholars
hold, indeed, that this primitive writing,
described in about 125 A.D. as a collection
of Sayings of the Lord in Hebrew, and
dated by the church fathers of the second
century, with the full approval of modern
critics, in the middle sixties, is only the
discourse nucleus of our so-called " Matthew," while the average layman naturally
makes no distinction between this and our
canonical Matthew.   But in either case,
the Sermon on the Mount is the heart of
it; so that the instinctive answer of layman and critic alike to the question, How
shall one come into most direct relation
with the Man of Nazareth through his
own words? will here be simply, Study
the Sermon on the Mount.

There is an additional appropriateness
of the subject in our case.   This lecture
comes, if I mistake not, as the conclusion
of a course of study in biblical literature.

You have doubtless followed the providential development of Israel's religious ideas, that were ultimately to impregnate the world, until at the opening of our era their entire content, whether priestly or prophetic, had come into formal concentration in the Law — the divine, sacred *Torah*, the one perfect revelation, as Israel esteemed it, of the will and character of God. There lay all the choicest product of the human thought of indefinite past centuries, as alternately suggested by the voice of God within, and pruned and corrected by the providence of God without. There it lay, as the seeds of the coming springtime lie hid in the hard, dry seed-pod through the storms and frosts of winter. The new religion was not new. Never did Jesus or his followers consent to be regarded as introducing a new religion. They were interpreters, not innovators; reformers, not iconoclasts. Matthew attaches to the opening and fundamental proposition of the great discourse, as he gives it, two sayings, which, even if we place them elsewhere * (partly on the authority of Luke, who gives the first in other context), may well be authentic, and in any case reflect as clearly as they do accurately the genuine conservatism of Jesus. "Verily I say unto you, until heaven and earth fail not one iota, nor turn of a letter shall fail from the law till all come to pass." This is the first, illustrating Jesus' respect for the revelation of the past. And as to the relative value of the work of destructive *vs.* constructive teaching Matthew adds a second : "Whosoever, therefore, shall 'loose' [show not to be binding] one of these least commandments, and teach men so [a necessary work since otherwise its performer would not be 'in the kingdom,' but one least worthy of all to be coveted], shall be called least in the Kingdom of God. But whoso shall do and teach them, he shall

* See Analytical Notes, Appendix A (4), p. 133, and compare Beyschlag, *New Test. Theol.*, I, p. 110.

be called great in the kingdom of God." *
Jesus, then, conceived the new as the
fruitage, the glorification, the transfiguration of the old. And that gospel,
which, as we saw, most clearly reflects the
standpoint of Jesus' own age and people,
distinctly gives expression to this conception, not merely in its repeated citation
of Jesus' teachings to this effect, but by
the fact that it begins the entire story of
his public career by the great discourse
we are to study, conspicuously placing
the Mount of Beatitudes over against the
Mount of the Law, and by the whole
arrangement of the material indicating
that this is to be considered what Paul
calls the "Law of Christ," what James,
that other Hebrew of Hebrews among
New Testament writers, speaks of as "the
perfect law," a mirror of moral perfection,
"the law of liberty," "the royal law,"
that is, the law of those who are children
of the King.

* See Text Critical Notes, Appendix A, p. 128.

Pardon me if I dwell for a moment on the fact; for it is not a mere coincidence that our study of Israel's Law, the outcome of its ages of development in religious thought, should conclude with that which to the view of a Jewish evangelist constitutes the corresponding element of Jesus' teaching. It is of importance in the method of study I propose to apply, whether this view of the evangelist is a mere fancy of his own, or whether Jesus himself actually framed a discourse having this character of the Renovation of the Law. I dwell on the question partly because very excellent scholars have strenuously denied it; * partly because if we can establish the probability of an actual discourse carefully and deliberately prepared by him from this point of view, we shall have in our hands the master

---

* *E.g.* Oscar Holtzmann in his *Leben Jesu*, 1901. See *per contra* H. J. Holtzmann in his *Neutestl. Thel.*, p. 131 : Das gesetzliche Judenthum bietet den positiven wie negativen Anknüpfungspunkt der Predigt Jesu.

key to many problems regarding the various types of early Christian apprehension of the gospel, Pauline, Jacobean, Johannine, their relation to one another and to their common authority. And this is of the utmost importance, because these are the channels, and the only channels, by which the gospel itself is transmitted to us.

Let us first do full justice to the objector. He points to the fact that in Luke, the Pauline evangelist, the Sermon on the Mount in every instance lacks those elements which in Matthew give it the distinctive character of a new *Torah*, a standard of righteousness (ethical and religious) offsetting the righteousness of scribes and Pharisees. He justly maintains that we must look to Paul, the radical opponent of legalism as legalism, no matter how high the standard, as truly reflecting the spirit of Jesus. The Palestinian mother-church, wedded as it was to its Judaistic particularism, and chary of the prerogatives of the seed of Abraham according to the flesh, chief among which was the having been "entrusted with the oracles of God," was slow to appreciate that the new wine must have new bottles. Our objector argues that the conception of Christianity as a *nova lex* was characteristic of the early catholic fathers, among whom it appears as a recrudescence of Judaism in Christian form. And if a conception be meant which treats the gospel exclusively or even predominantly as a *nova lex*, it is rightly designated post-Pauline. After the death of Paul, the plain and easy notion of legalism crept back. Religion became again a matter of requirement and reward. The *quid pro quo* system, by which scribism had caricatured the Old Testament into, You do this for God, and God will do what you want for you, returned to power.* This tendency in the early

* Cf. H. J. Holtzmann, *Neutestl. Theol.*, p. 158: Selbst die entschiedenen Worte [Jesu], welche die letzten

church consciously to undo the work of Paul we may designate neo-legalism.   And it had historical reality.   We must grant to the objector that even our Gospel of Matthew already shows traces of the tendency, as when borrowing from Mk. 10 : 17–31 the story of the rich Pharisee who asked Jesus what good work he must do,* it removes

Tage brachten, Tempelsturz und neuer Bund, vermochten in dem Bewusstsein der Urgemeinde den Eindruck der viel längeren Zeit nicht aufzuheben, welche vorangegangen war.

* The relation of dependence is here obvious as soon as the parallels are brought into juxtaposition.   Besides the now generally admitted fact that our first evangelist borrows practically the whole of his narrative material from Mark, we have in the particular instance of Mk. 10: 17–22 = Mt. 19: 16–22 two differences wherein the change of the Markan form to the Matthæan is most natural but the reverse process inconceivable.   (1) Jesus' disclaimer in Mark of the scribe's epithet, " Why callest thou me good ? " is changed in Matthew to " Why askest thou me about goodness ? "   Yet even Matthew leaves the second clause, " One only is good," substantially as it was.   (2) Matthew's version assimilates the commandments very freely cited by Mark to the exact language of the Old Testament and then supplements them with the new commandment of Jesus.   Surely

Jesus' disclaimer of the title "good" in the sense of having merit with God, and changes the contrast Jesus draws between a goodness which consists in mere observance of the common rules of morality in the hope of reward, and a "faith" which has renounced all to die for God's kingdom. In the Matthæan form this becomes a weak *addition* of one to the other. But in its original Markan form this story might be said to give Mark's equivalent to the Sermon on the Mount. For by the relation of incident rather than discourse it contrasts the righteousness of Jesus and his followers, who have no "goodness" save the gift of His Spirit who alone is "good," but having left all are now about to give their lives for the gospel, with the "righteousness" of scribes and Pharisees, based as it was on a punctilious casuistry which seeks to "inherit eternal life." In form, Jesus seems to

one cannot remain in doubt here as to which form is secondary.

accede to the Pharisee's request for a process of acquiring merit, and so having a
claim on God for reward. In reality
legalism is left helpless. There is no
polemic, no *anti*-legalism, as in Paul. But
the victory of faith over works is just as
absolute. The Pharisee is left as completely as the publican at the mercy of
God. This is the paradox of Jesus'
legalism, which is really the opposite.
We may call it quasi-legalistic. And it
must be admitted that our first gospel
misses the point when it makes Jesus
simply commend the young ruler for his
strict obedience to the ten commandments
(supplemented here by the Christian summary, Thou shalt love thy neighbor as
thyself), assure him that if he does this
he shall live, and then add, but if thou
wouldst attain the highest grade of
righteousness,* "go sell all thou hast and

* Εἰ θέλεις τέλειος εἶναι. The same word, τέλειος
"complete," employed in the Greek mysteries of the
"adept," is used by this evangelist to sum up Christ's

give to the poor." This representation of the gospel is simply legalism keyed up to a little higher pitch. What Paul would have said to it we may guess from his great chapter on the *charism* of the spirit of love: "Though I bestow all my goods to feed the poor, and give my body to be burned, but have not the divine gift of the spirit of love — *it is nothing.*" But it does not follow that Jesus was legalistic because Matthew shows certain tendencies of the sort. Our excellent Jewish Christian first evangelist has no idea that in making these slight changes in the story of Mark he is antagonizing Paul. No more than has James, when he insists that a man is not "justified by faith apart from works," — a flat contradiction of Rom. 3 : 28, — but that he must *add* the one to the other. Still less does our first evangelist

teaching of the new righteousness in the Sermon on the Mount (Mt. 5 : 48). The corresponding passage in Luke (6 : 36) has οἰκτίρμονες "merciful."

realize that he is leaving out the most vital element in the teaching of Jesus, that *righteousness is not merit,** but a being imbued with the Spirit of Him who alone is "good." He misunderstands Mark as "James" misunderstands Romans. Like the excellent converted Pharisees of Jerusalem in the 50's and 60's, like their successors among the catholic fathers, he finds himself incapable of outgrowing all at once an inborn, inbred legalism.

In other words, our first evangelist has still somewhat to learn of Christ from Paul. For him Christianity is a sublimated, transfigured Judaism. It is " the law and the prophets " in their essential content and fulfilment, and nothing more (Mt. 7 : 12

---

* The saying in Lk. 17 : 7–10, " When ye have done all the things commanded you, say, We are unprofitable servants: we have done that which it was our duty to do," puts Jesus' attitude toward the notion of righteousness as merit, having a claim to reward, in his own inimitable way. The parable of the Unequal Wage, Mt. 20 : 1–16, is aimed at the same Pharisaic error.

cf. Lk. 6 : 31). Now since we have reason
to know on independent grounds that
Mark's representation of this incident and
its accompanying teaching is more original
and correct than Matthew's, and moreover
are aware from the very possibility of Paulinism that Jesus did not teach a mere re-
formed legalism,* the conclusion could not
be escaped, if the fundamental character
of the Sermon on the Mount prove really
neo-legalistic, that the composition as a
whole, however genuine its principal elements, belongs to the evangelist. It would
therefore represent not so much the teaching of Jesus himself as that of the early
church of Palestine such as it is described
by James in Acts 21 : 20, "Myriads of
believing Jews all zealots for the Law."
Its apparent form of a new *Torah*, a more
refined and loftier system of ethical requirement, would also then be due to the
evangelist and not to Jesus.

This argument of criticism is an ex-

* See also the note above.

tremely weighty one, which cannot be dismissed until full justice has been done it, and this may well demand readjustment and modification of accepted views, even if they be retained as a whole. We shall return to it later.

Pass now to a second consideration. It is sufficient merely to attempt in imagination to realize by what means long discourses of Jesus could be perpetuated unwritten for at least a generation, to perceive that we have no right to expect the preservation of whole addresses or sermons. Even were we to take the three chapters of Matthew which correspond to the thirty-three verses of Luke, as giving us the great address just as delivered, the whole of this longest sermon would occupy in delivery only a few minutes of time, whereas we know Jesus often taught for hours. Parables could be remembered, epigrammatic answers to interlocutors, apophthegms, principles applied to the solution of current questions of religion,

c

patriotism, and duty.   But even the memory of a trained disciple of the rabbis refused to carry sermons and addresses, and the supposed examples afforded by the New Testament have repeatedly turned out on closer scrutiny to be of the usual type of reported addresses in secular historians of that era, viz., compositions of the author out of the best material at his command, intended to represent, as well as the material permitted, what the speaker *would* have said.   The evidence of this lies in many cases in the circumstances of the interview, which are often such as to preclude other authority for the author's report than hearsay and conjecture.   So the dialogue of Jesus with Pilate, Jn. 18: 32–38, speech of Gamaliel to the Sanhedrin, Acts 5 : 34–40, letter of Lysias to Felix, Acts 23 : 25–30, and the like.   In other cases additional evidence appears in the language and style, as where the Johannine discourses are indistinguishable in style and character from the epistles of

John, or as in the speeches of Acts, which are at least shaped by the author to his purpose, and display his characteristic diction. Even the sermon of Jesus in the synagogue at Nazareth, wherewith our third evangelist opens his account of the public ministry, while made up of authentic material,* is unmistakably adapted to the purpose of the historian who relates the Redeemer's rejection by his own people and subsequent welcome by the Gentiles, even as it had been foretold by the prophets, rather than the purpose in Jesus' mind when he addressed his fellow-towns-

---

* The *logia* (" divine utterances ") of Jesus were placed on a superhuman plane in even the earliest time (1 Cor. 7: 10, 12, 25). Reverence for them was too great to admit of the kind of composition employed elsewhere. But composition by agglutination, *i.e.* the joining together of *logia* separately transmitted, is a demonstrable phenomenon of the gospels and a constant practice of the fathers, as in Clement of Rome, *ad Cor.* 13:2. An instructive illustration of a saying (originally the answer to a question) transformed by the evangelist into the subject-matter of a sermon, is found in Mk. 1: 7-8, displacing as it does the real *preaching* of John, Mt. 3: 7-10, 12=Lk. 3: 7-9, 17; cf. Jn. 1: 19-25 and Lk. 3: 15.

men.   The constant reiteration of this
theme of the obduracy of Israel compelling
the heralds of the gospel to "turn to the
Gentiles" throughout the third gospel and
Acts shows that the quotation from Isaiah,
and subsequent justification of the preaching of the gospel to the Gentiles by the
examples of Elijah and Elisha, in Lk.
4: 16–30, cannot be attributed to Jesus
under just this form and these circumstances, though they may well be authentic
utterances.   This being, then, at least a
possible method of the evangelists, we
cannot rule out of court the view that the
Sermon on the Mount has received the
form of a connected discourse simply by
the aggregation of remembered sayings of
Jesus, in later times and for catechetic
purposes.   We have, then, much to con-
cede to the objector under this second
head also.   For (1) we have *a priori* no
right to expect connected reports of sermons; (2) those we appear to have are
certainly in many cases compositions out

of more or less authentic material; (3) the main course of criticism up to the present has been rightly analytical rather than synthetic, because the most approved results go to show that the earliest processes of gospel composition tended toward aggregation rather than disintegration. In other words, all we know by tradition, as well as by scrutiny of the completed work goes to show effort on the part of primitive compilers of the Lord's sayings to *form* connections, even where they did not exist, rather than a disposition to *break up* existing contexts and connections. This of course is no more than we should expect, but it imposes upon us the task of analysis in order to get at the original.

Thus appears a second weighty objection to the authenticity of the Sermon on the Mount as a connected discourse. And this, too, must be treated as carefully and as justly as the first.

Finally we have evidence — conclusive unless we reject the explicit statements of Luke — that about one-fourth of the Matthæan discourse consists of teachings uttered on other occasions; and this testimony of Luke, as we shall see, is corroborated by the internal evidence of the teachings themselves, which agree much better with the circumstances under which Luke declares them to have been uttered, than with the Matthæan setting. Indeed, the removal of them often restores the original discourse to greater symmetry, beauty, and intelligibility.

This third objection is fatal to any attempt to vindicate the entire Matthæan composition as a transcript, or even synopsis of the actual address. The so-called Sermon on the Mount certainly contains, at least, a very considerable element of agglutinated fragments. Conceivably it might be wholly made up of them. Actually, I am convinced that it does not, but represents a real discourse of Jesus substantially of the character represented by our first gospel, in spite of all discounts necessary to be made on the score of the critical objections above noted. Not only so, but I believe it to be possible to give strict critical demonstration of an underlying, connected discourse whose subject was the new *Torah* of the righteousness of the kingdom of God. And this discourse, if not directly derived in this particular form from Jesus himself, is at least decidedly older than either our first or third gospel, so much older as to go back beyond all reasonable doubt to the time when many still survived who remembered the actual preaching of Jesus.

For let us first briefly review the objections, and see just how much and how little is really implied, and afterward I will state some of the reasons which lead me to the conclusion stated.

The first objection confronts us with an "if," which nothing but critical scrutiny of the material will determine. *If*

the fundamental character of the Sermon
on the Mount is neo-legalistic, we must
regard it as a composition of the evangelist whose modification of the Markan
incident of the rich young man so
significantly takes this direction. It is
the word " fundamental " which must
bear the stress. Neo-legalistic touches
here and there,* especially such as do
not appear in the Lucan version, may
easily be accounted for as supplied by
the evangelist without affecting the main
course of thought. Nay, more. If, as
may often be the case, the intrusive
character of these additions becomes
apparent from their disagreement with
the sense of the context, the argument
may be inverted. The very fact that
the evangelist deems it needful to introduce modifying clauses and paragraphs
of the neo-legalistic type goes to show
that the material he thus alters was

---

* *E.g.* Mt. 5 : 16 καλὰ ἔργα, 18-19, 32 παρεκτὸς λόγου
πορνείας, 7 : 12ᵇ.

either anti-legalistic, or at least not legal-istic enough to meet his views. Now in the course of our review we shall find repeatedly that it is not the funda-mental but the overlying elements, modi-fying clauses, appended qualifications, which display the neo-legalistic tendency; whereas the fundamental course of thought in the discourse as a whole is exactly parallel to the teaching of the Markan incident of the rich young man: righteousness is not a store of accumu-lated merits, but self-surrender to the inworking of the Spirit of the divine goodness. This quasi-legalism, as we have designated it, is not indeed the same as Paulinism, but it rests upon the same doctrine of *faith* as the one thing needful. It involves that mysticism of Jesus without which neither the Pauline nor the Johannine teaching could have ventured to call itself by his name. To this first objection, therefore, we may answer: A neo-legalistic element is unde-

niably present in the Matthæan Sermon
on the Mount; but so far is this from
representing the main course of thought
that its conflict therewith rather tends
to prove an underlying discourse whose
character could not be fairly regarded
as more than quasi-legalistic.

But it is presented as a second objection that the actual teaching of Jesus
was in the form of " brief and concise
utterances " on the testimony of very
ancient tradition * as well as the ordinary
representation of the synoptic gospels ;
so that we have no right to expect the
report of extended discourses, but on the
contrary are taught by all experience
that the supposed extended discourses of
the New Testament are either free compositions of the historian, or formed by
agglutination.   We are also directed to
the *Pirke Aboth*, or " Sayings of the
Jewish Fathers," a substantially contem-

* The words quoted are from Justin Martyr.   First
Apology, xiv, ca. 155 A.D.

porary record of teachings of the rabbis
of Jesus' time and earlier, as the closest
parallel to the earliest gospel writings.
These apophthegms and sententious sayings represent, we are told, not only the
form of the earliest records — the Oxy-
rhynchus fragment corroborates this view
— but the form of the teaching of Jesus
itself. But at this point we must demur.
The example of the *Pirke Aboth* is
highly instructive as to the probable
nature of the first evangelic composition
of which we have record, the Hebrew
(Aramaic) *Logia* of Jesus by the Apostle
Matthew; but it suggests the wrong analogy for the principal public utterances
of Jesus. We should look rather to the
Old Testament prophets, and to John the
Baptist, their then living representative,
for types of that Teacher who stirred
the multitudes with amazement because
he spoke " with authority, and *not* as
the scribes." John the Baptist, Jesus,
and the Apostles were in their mode of

utterance not scribes but "*preachers*," and we have accordingly no word better fitted than the word "sermon," used in its noblest sense, to describe the kind of discourse Jesus gave when he went round about the cities and villages of Galilee teaching, healing, and, on the the Sabbaths, *preaching in their synagogues*.

Undoubtedly the great majority of the recorded teachings of our gospels are of the other type, the occasional pithy saying, apophthegm, or wise and witty retort, the parable and illustration, or remembered fragment of consecutive discourse. But to take rabbinic teaching, even at its best, as the type mainly followed by Jesus, is to ignore one of the fundamental distinctions of the age; or rather to choose the very opposite of the true alternative.

The teaching in the synagogues of Jesus' time was of two types, designated respectively *halachah* and *haggadah*. The former was authoritative and legal. The scribe, or lawyer, who gave it, simply expounded and applied the precepts of the law.* Of such casuistry, precedent and case-law, consists the great body of the Talmud, and Jesus, who by courtesy was addressed as "rabbi," was often appealed to for decisions in this field; whether to entrap him, as in the incident of the denarius, and the law of divorce, or in good

---

* A modern critic of eminence depicts the great rabbi in the synagogue, sitting in meditative silence in the midst of his awe-struck disciples. After long periods of silence the great man raises his head. He will not use the vulgar tongue of "the people of the land," but whispers his weighty decision in the ear of his "minister" in the sacred Hebrew. And the *targum* man, or interpreter (*anglice* dragoman), thereupon proclaims it to the attentive congregation. As an illustration of *halachic* teaching this is most serviceable and furnishes an admirable commentary on the saying, "What ye have heard in the ear proclaim upon the housetops." But as an illustration of the public teaching of Jesus, it would be absolutely misleading. Equally incredible in my judgment is the view of certain leading critics that either Jesus or the earliest compilers of his teachings should have copied the rabbinic affectation of employing the Hebrew language, unintelligible as it was to the masses.

faith, as when asked, "Who is my 'neigh-bor'?" or "What is the chief command-ment?" But Jesus *never consents to enter* this field of *halachah*. It is one which he turns over absolutely to the lawyers by profession, "the scribes who sit in Moses' seat." He *declines* to teach ethics or casu-istry, save as involved in his simple mes-sage of religion. He declines to refer to authorities. In the language of his con-temporaries his teaching was not *halachah*, but *haggadah;* not law, but *preaching;* and in the haggadic style, accordingly, must we look for the rhetorical forms to which those employed by Jesus are more nearly allied. Edification was the one supreme object of *haggadah*, and its range was as unlimited as its authority was un-defined. Its very name denotes the "folk-tale" or "story"; its origin was in the democratic synagogue, not in the aristo-cratic schools of the temple. No pre-cedent or authority needed to be cited, no literary expedient of allegory, fiction, or

legend was excluded.   Inevitably the synagogue harangue on the Sabbath tended
toward this character, rather than its alternative, most of all in unsophisticated
Galilee; for who could listen for hours
on end to the dreary casuistry of the
lawyers?   And Jesus was not only a
preacher, but an impassioned, and, in the
loftiest sense of the word, a popular
preacher.   Is it, then, so incredible that,
in addition to the mass of sententious
utterances, apophthegms, and answers recorded in our gospels, there should also
remain some traces of connected discourse
— of preaching?   We may not, indeed,
expect more than the briefest fragments
of any such address; but may there not
be enough to form some outline?   Must
all the evidences of logical and rhetorical
arrangement, displayed in such passages as
the eulogy of John the Baptist (Mt. 11:
7–19), the discourses on the Sign of Jonah
(Lk. 11 : 27–32), and on the True Content
of Life (Lk. 12: 13–31), be attributed to

mere editors and collectors of sayings? Criticism has, indeed, concerned itself up to now for the most part with analysis, and rightly so. It has won unquestionable results in disproof of certain attempted syntheses of early gospel writers; in many instances our evangelists have formed, or taken over, combinations of sayings which demonstrably were not uttered in this relation or connection. But while the conscious and direct effort of proto-evangelists was doubtless directed toward combination, we have evidence no less conclusive of an unconscious and indirect tendency toward disintegration. Their very effort to recombine is evidence that they were aware of the fragmentary character of their material. Often it gave mere salient points retained by memory from larger structures. Moreover, these very attempts, when unsuccessful, will have often produced still further disintegration. Of this the Sermon on the Mount itself will furnish many an example. And this imposes upon us the task of synthesis as imperatively as that of analysis. Doubtless the task is precarious. Doubtless analysis and reconstruction of the documentary sources should precede attempts to restore the very utterances themselves. But are not some steps already possible that shall be both trustworthy and critical? To this the answer must be found in the attempt itself.

Finally, we had as a third objection to the discovery of any authentic discourse to which the name Sermon on the Mount was justly applicable, the disagreement of the two authorities who report it. In Matthew the main thread of logical connection, so far as traceable, is the contrast of the righteousness of the Law with the righteousness of the Kingdom. In Luke two-thirds of this material does not appear at all, while two-thirds or more of the remainder is related, in most cases, with every evidence of correctness, as uttered on other occasions.

D

In weighing the effect of this objection
we have already conceded the evidence
of agglutination.   A very considerable
element of the Matthæan Sermon on the
Mount must on the evidence of Luke be
admitted to result from mistaken synthesis
on the part of the compiler.   But because
some of his syntheses are mistaken must
all be necessarily so?   Will the disagreement of an independent witness disprove,
and the agreement not corroborate?   But
our final answer to this and all other objections can only be by actual comparison
and cross-examination of the two witnesses.   Then, if after all needful deduc-
tions and corrections of the one report by
the other have been made, the unassail-
ble remnant shall still appear not less, but
more, logically and rhetorically connected
than before ; if it be more than ever like
a literary unit of connected discourse, less
than ever like a mere agglomeration of
sayings, the very divergence and indepen-
dence of the witnesses will strengthen the

proof that this unity is not artificial, but original ; that it goes far back into the age of living first-hand tradition, if not to the great Preacher himself.

So much as to the objections, which we have endeavored to estimate at their true value ; no more, no less.

I have now to present three reasons for my conviction that Matthew, however incorrect in the admission of many large masses of discourse uttered on other occasions, is in his general representation correct.

There was a real sermon, a Sermon on the Mount, a discourse of Jesus to his disciples, worthy to be called the New Torah of the Kingdom of God ; because in it he set forth, with that clear consistency of thought and integrity of style so characteristic of the parables, the relation of morality and religion in the coming kingdom, to that of which the scribes and Pharisees were respectively the theoretical and practical exponents.   Thus the special

rhetorical form in which the discourse
is cast, an antitype to the Law of Moses,
is not something *created* by our evangelist, but rather, *turned to account* by
him; for, when we inquire as to the real
doctrinal import, the neo-legalistic tendency appears nowhere but in superficial
touches.   The discourse as a whole, if
not positively anti-legalistic is at least
non-legalistic.

My first reason for justifying to this
extent the representation of our first evangelist is chiefly negative. We must account
for the absence from the discourse in
Luke's version (Lk. 6:20–49) of all that
pertains to the contrast between the new
righteousness and the old.   But to understand this we have only to remember, first,
that Luke is almost certainly addressing
Gentiles, who had small interest in the
mere relation of the teaching of Jesus to
what "they of old time" had said, or the
righteousnesses esteemed by scribe and
Pharisee. His readers wanted simply the

positive content of Jesus' requirement.*
Second, we must remember the strong
anti-Judaism of this writer, as evinced in
Acts, which might lead him to neglect the
antithesis of Law and Gospel. Third, we
have only to compare his very cavalier
treatment of a kindred section of Mark,
whose gospel we know lay before him.
I mean the section on Jesus' conflict with
"the scribes who came down from Jerusalem" about ceremonial washings, the
traditions of the elders, and the distinctions of clean and unclean meats (Mk. 7:
1–23), all of which Luke practically elimi-
nates. We see it then to have been the ac-

---

* Our third gospel is often spoken of as a Gentile gospel, largely on the assumption that the tradition associ-
ating it with the name of the Gentile Luke is correct.
On this point we make no assumption (see Bacon, *Introd. to N. T. Lit.*, pp. 211–229). On the contrary the
sections *peculiar* to Luke are more strongly Palestinian,
Petrine, and Jewish-Christian than any other element of
the New Testament. But excisions are made (*e.g.* of
Mk. 7 : 24–30), and misunderstandings occur (Lk.
11 : 39 ; cf. Mt. 23: 25 and 2: 22 (?)), which suggest
rather a Gentile destination and Gentile compiler.

tual practice of this evangelist to strike out
matter which, as he looked at it, only concerned Jesus' relation to Jewish law.* Thus
Luke's omissions are not unaccountable.

But there is more. Evidence exists in
Luke's own report that this part of the
Sermon on the Mount really was once
present in the source which he employed.
Turn to Lk. 6:27, and ask yourselves
why it should begin, "*But I say* unto
you," † without something before it corresponding to Matthew's antithesis of what
"they of old time" had said. More significant still, how comes it that the striking
thought and phrase on ground of which

---

* Compare also the reduced dimensions of the Woes
against scribes and Pharisees in Mt. 23, as given in
Lk. 11, and of the Warning against their teaching
Mt. 16:5–12 = Mk. 8: 13–21, in Lk. 12:1.

† The Greek, Ἀλλὰ ὑμῖν λέγω τοῖς ἀκούουσιν, " But to
you that hear, I say," places the contrast otherwise than
the English would suggest. But the distinction between
the absent rich, full, well spoken of, and present poor,
empty, persecuted, impresses one as forced upon the connection rather than original. It was needless to specify
that the speaker addressed those present, not the absent.

the acts of piety, almsgiving, prayer, fasting done from ostentation are denied any credit with God — ἀπέχουσι τὸν μισθὸν αὐτῶν, "they have in full their reward" * — is the same thought and phrase on ground of which they that are "rich and increased in goods, and have need of nothing" are denied a share in the kingdom, if both are not from the same mind? Yet one is the Matthæan refrain of the antitheses on the true worship (Mt. 6: 1–18), which do not appear in Luke; and the other is the Lukan burden of the Woes (Lk. 6: 24–26), which do not appear in Matthew. Both sections must be authentic, or the characteristic thought and expression would not appear on both sides; for Matthew, in the form that we have it, was almost certainly unknown to

* The recently discovered contemporary papyri from the Fayoum admirably illustrate the peculiar use of this term, ἀπέχουσι, translated by the Revisers, "they have received." It is the technical term by which one receipts in full for a loan or bill. See Deissmann, *Bible Studies*, p. 229.

Luke.* We are compelled to assume a common source which included elements omitted first by Matthew, then by Luke.

My second reason for indorsing the title " The New Torah " may sound somewhat *a priori* in character, until you know the facts. But let me state it first. I do not believe that the Reformer, who, after his triumphant entry into Jerusalem, began his programme of openly Messianic activity † with the cleansing of the temple, accompanied as it was by the great saying about rebuilding it in three days, can have failed at a much earlier period to make full, clear, and formal definition to at least the inner circle of his disciples of his relation to that institution which

* See my *Introduction to the New Testament*, 1900, p. 180.

† That is, the final Passover week. The ministry previously had not been *openly* Messianic (Mt. 16 : 17, 20). Could we suppose with the fourth evangelist that Jesus' Messianic claims were openly declared from the beginning, his placing of the cleansing of the temple might be admissible. But this is impossible.

to them was even greater, and far more closely related to their religious life; I mean the Law. There were certain great, stereotyped Messianic expectations of Jesus' time, only partly justified by Scripture, it is true, and in other respects ill-befitting the kingdom he proclaimed, to which Jesus yet clearly adapted himself and gave fulfilment, albeit a fulfilment so much more spiritual than the current idea as to meet but small acceptance. Such was the very conception of Christhood itself. It is by no means Jesus' own term for the part he felt called on to play. He uses the term but three times in all, and then as it were under protest.* He is the Christ, indeed, but not what men mean by the term. He gives it a new sense. He knows himself the Son of God, but that, too, not in the accepted sense. He calls himself the Son of Man.

* For the real significance of Jesus' reply to the adjuration of the high priest, " Art thou the Christ ?" — σὺ εἶπας, see Thayer, in *Journ. of Bibl. Lit.*, 1894.

So also with the current ideas of the
redemption to be brought in. Perhaps
the most widespread figure by which it
was expressed was the conception of the
great Messianic feast. This also Jesus
spiritualizes (Mt. 4 : 4), or turns into a
feeding of the world with his doctrine
(Jn. 6 : 26–58 ; cf. Mt. 16 : 12). Jesus, we
see, was too wise to begin his reformatory
career with open claims of a Messianic
office whose nature all would misunder-
stand. But it is impossible to suppose
that he began it without a clear notion
of what he himself meant by it, or without
a full realization that it implied a recast-
ing of the most fundamental institutions
of Israel; in particular, a new conception
of the Kingdom of God, or reign of
Messiah. Common sense thus required
him to begin by teaching in what new
sense these great ideas of the popular
hope and faith must be understood. Now,
if you have read something of the literature which is just beginning to reveal

to us the religious conceptions of Jesus'
time from Jewish sources, I mean such
books as Weber's *Lehre des Talmud* and
R. H. Charles's *Eschatology*, you will find
that there were two expectations of Messiah profoundly established in the popular faith, having genuine root in the
great prophecies of the past, and at the
same time of such a nature that they
could not but appeal to Jesus as at least
in some sense justifiable. It will be a
very helpful illustration of what we may
term the pedagogic method of Jesus, to
observe how he dealt with these two
current particulars of the general Messianic hope; both of them of larger and
deeper significance than that of the Messianic feast already referred to. One of
these two maintained that foremost among
the achievements of Messiah would be the
rebuilding of Jerusalem and the temple.
Weber, in § 83 of his book, cites a multitude of passages from the Talmud illustrative of the expectation. First, such

as relate to the city, based, of course, on
Isaiah and Ezekiel, and constantly recall-
ing to us the picture of the New Jerusalem of Revelation ; and, second, an equal
number regarding the similar renovation
of the temple, which is, of course, to
every Jew, the glory of Jerusalem. The
targum on Is. 53 : 5 already declares that
Messiah will rebuild the sanctuary, and
later writings enlarge upon its surpassing
glory. The pre-Christian book of Enoch
similarly enlarges on this Messianic renewal of the temple. Not improbably
the disciples may have had it in mind
when they pointed with pride to the
goodly stones of the temple of Herod.
And Jesus, as we have seen, did not turn
a deaf ear to this Messianic expectation.
The great symbolic act of purifying the
temple defined his position with regard
to it, but not without an accompanying
statement in explicit terms. He predicted
the overthrow of that "temple built with
hands," but promised that "in three

days" he would replace it by a spiritual temple, world-wide, eternal, in which true worshippers should render spiritual sacrifice to the Father of all. Thereupon, down all the succession of Christian preachers and writers, Stephen, Paul, Peter, John, and long after among the fathers, reëchoes the great saying of Jesus on the living "temple not built with hands" of the Messianic kingdom.

Similar is his treatment of the other expectation, regarding a still more fundamental institution of Israel. No less explicit and positive than the expectation regarding the temple was the popular faith of Jesus' day that Messiah when he came would reconstruct the Law. The very scribes, untiring as they were in their exaggerated laudation of its perfections, were abundantly conscious of the need of interpretation. This need they sometimes expressed by declaring with R. Chija of Is. 53 : 5 (the same passage applied to the rebuilding of the temple): "This relates to the days of Messiah. A great thing will then occur. The *Torah* will be as if new; it will be renewed for Israel." Sometimes they spoke as if the transformation were to be still more radical: "The Holy One, blessed be he, will sit and teach [*darash*] a new *Torah*, which he will give through Messiah." But the expression *darash*, the technical term for exposition,* shows that what is really predicted is only such illuminative interpretation, that the Law would seem new, transfigured, glorified. In this sense the Christ was called in Jewish Christian circles the "true Prophet," the second Moses.† Even in the days of Judas Maccabæus they laid up for his coming the stones of the altar defiled by Antiochus Epiphanes, not knowing what to do with them; and, as we

---

* Literally "tread out," a figure derived from the process of threshing by the feet of oxen. Paul (1 Cor. 9 : 9) assumes that Dt. 25 : 4 must apply principally to the human *darshan* (*i.e.* "treader out") rather than to literal oxen, on grounds similar to Lk. 12 : 24.

† So in *Clem. Homilies* and *Recognitions, passim.*

know, the Samaritan woman herself believes that the end of controversy as between Jerusalem and Mount Gerizim will be "when Messiah cometh, who will tell us all things." Rightly or wrongly the shepherdless sheep of Israel looked forward with longing to Messiah as the great Interpreter of Scripture, the "Renewer of the Law" — so they called him *
— and such an expectation we have a right to assume Jesus would not disappoint.

It is true that this is *a priori* reasoning, by which it would be hopeless, in the absence of actual reported utterances, to establish more than the possibility that Jesus *might*, even at a very early period of his ministry in Galilee, have drawn a detailed comparison between the present *Torah* and the *Torah* of the age to come. But it is precisely this which we are called upon to prove. The reported utterance exists. The gospels report a discourse

* See the passage cited below from *Test. of Levi*, 16.

of this type. But the possibility of such a discourse is denied, on the ground that Jesus could not, at so early a period in his ministry, have assumed to legislate as Messiah, and the existence of the report is explained as due to the conviction of the evangelists that Jesus was the Messiah, their mistaken inference that therefore he must from the outset have promulgated the Messianic Torah, and their ability to put together from the occasional sayings of Jesus an agglomeration sufficient to bear the title.

Now this objection is removed as soon as we reflect that the utterance of the supposed discourse is a very different matter, as regards the inference to be drawn as to the speaker's personality, from such an act as the purifying of the temple, which instantly called forth the demand, " By what authority doest thou these things ? " It indeed the discourse were rightly described as the promulgation of the Messianic Law, if the speaker really placed himself in the attitude, not of *declaring the nature of the law that will prevail* in the kingdom of heaven, but of *personally legislating* to this effect, then the objection would hold. As it is, there is nothing belonging to the genuine substance of the reported discourse which goes beyond the general nature of Jesus' teaching in Galilee as reported by all the Synoptists. It is indeed a teaching of " authority " unlike that of the scribes, and so well calculated to rouse the amazement of the hearers; but not beyond that of the preaching of the Baptist. It is the authority of " a mighty prophet," announcing now not merely that " the kingdom of heaven is at hand," but announcing also its nature, and the character of its laws and institutions. Yet no one need infer more as to the nature of the speaker than that he is " Jeremias or one of the prophets," or perhaps " Elias that was for to come," or even " John the Baptist risen from the dead." It is simply in line with the general message of " the

E

prophet of Nazareth," how that, "the time is fulfilled and the kingdom at hand,"·and with the parables by which he defined its character, that to those who listened to his authoritative summons to "believe the glad tidings" and order their lives accordingly, he should also set forth the nature and principles of its Law.   Understand the Sermon on the Mount as we have shown and will show that it must be understood, as the utterance not of a legislator but a *prophet* of the kingdom, and the objection disappears.   Add now the consideration adduced that expectations of his hearers which must needs have appealed to Jesus as legitimate, loudly called for an immediate declaration on this point of the relation of the New Torah to that of which Scribe and Pharisee were the exponents, and the argument is reversed.   We should rather be greatly surprised if our authorities did not report utterances of the Master, clearly genuine, in which his followers' expectation on this point was met.

But if met, was it in so obscure a way, that only the later speculation of the church, turning back and reflecting on his teachings, would at last realize that its "new law" was already given? Or did he meet it as clearly and manifestly as that regarding the temple, setting in contrast the standard of righteousness which must prevail in the kingdom he declared "at hand" with the standards of those who sat in Moses' seat? Certainly the early church thought its Master had proclaimed a new *Torah.* We have not only James with his "royal law," his "law of liberty" proclaimed by Christ, not only Barnabas, with his opposition of "the new law of our Lord Jesus Christ; which is without the yoke of constraint" to the Law of Moses; not only the *nova lex* of the catholic fathers, but writings of the primitive Jewish church like the *Testament of Levi,* which lay hold on the very language of scribal expectation, placing in the mouth of the patriarch the prediction " The man who *reneweth the law* in the power of the Highest ye will call a deceiver, and at last will slay him."

On this question, whether, and to what extent the tradition of the church is justified, nothing will enlighten us save a detailed scrutiny of the reported discourse itself, as its own internal sequence of thought reveals its purpose. And we must distinguish here between the internal evidence and the view of the reporter; for the evangelist, as some argue to whom we have already referred, might have been led by his innate habit of thought to cast his great initial discourse of Jesus in this form. So far as possible, then, we must get back of all editorial work. We must put together all we can learn from the three synoptic sources regarding the occasion and content, and draw from all sources our conclusion on the question: What was the Sermon on the Mount in its own inherent literary structure and didactic purpose ?

But to answer this question is not only to decide whether or not there was a discourse of approximately the character we have been accustomed to believe; it is at the same time to interpret. We shall be getting at one of the most important, if not the most important, of Jesus' public utterances; and in proportion to its importance, and our success in getting at *his* point of view, *his own* words and thought, we shall also be achieving our supreme purpose of knowing this Son of Man, not by what we are told about him, but because we have heard him ourselves.

I crave your patience with many preliminaries. There remains still, after the formulation of our problem, a word as to method. For the method, after all, is more than the results of its application in any particular instance. And I must not only define, but possibly even defend; for that which I propose to apply — to some extent have already applied — is to many an object of profound distrust and suspicion.   It is the method of the higher criticism.

It is a pity that any method of Bible study — a process for getting at the real significance of Scripture — should be an object of suspicion to godly people. However, novelty, especially in matters of religion, cannot expect to pass unchallenged. Yet ask yourselves this question : What interest can a man possibly take in investigating the origins of the biblical writings who has no interest in the writings themselves ? If scholars whose standing and influence, if not their very livelihood, depend on the continued interest and respect accorded to the writings of the Canon, to say nothing of the personal enthusiasm they manifest, are willing to devote a lifetime to the exploration of the obscure problems of the growth of this literature, is it not reasonable to suppose that they do so as a rule in the conviction that the real value of the Bible will thereby be enhanced ?   Is it

probable that they are all trying, in metaphorical phrase, to saw off the branch they
hang to ? So much as to motive. I leave
the witness of the many who declare this
method to have been an unveiling of the
Scriptures to them to speak for the results.

As to definition. The higher criticism
is the complement of the lower, or textual,
which deals with the transmission and dis-
semination of the sacred text, after it left
the hand which gave it its ultimate form
as a literary product. The textual critic
asks : "What was originally written ? "
The higher critic asks : How came it to
be written ? When ? why ? and by whom ?

Like every product of human effort,
these writings had a history of their formation as well as of their distribution. To
stop arbitrarily at the point where the
author gave his work to the public, is as
though one should leave off with botany
at the surface of the ground, and declare
the root and seed life of the plant an inscrutable mystery. Still more absurd if

this author employed the work of prede-
cessors in the field, as Luke for one has
done, on the evidence of his own report
(Lk. 1 : 1).   Back of the work of historian,
compiler, letter-writer, editor, with his pen,
lies his work as an accumulator of materi-
als, oral or written.   Other equally important factors are his own personality,
purpose, mental history and propensity,
his environment, and the occasion of his
writing, the effect of the thought of others
on his own, whether as antagonist or perhaps as correspondents.*   Knowledge of all
this is as indispensable to an understanding of the true significance of writings, as
knowledge of what happens under the soil
to an understanding of plants; and from
its relation to textual study the method is
called the higher (*i.e.* remoter, antecedent)
criticism.

But it is said knowledge on these subjects is impossible, and, moreover, the

* As the Corinthians, to whose letter (1 Cor. 7 : 1)
Paul is replying in our First Corinthians.

processes employed and results announced are very obnoxious to devout conviction. As to the possibility or impossibility of ascertaining something here, all we need say is, that is just the question to be determined ; the process and evidence are public ; if results seem meagre or ill-supported, let them go for what they are worth. They do not stand on authority, but on their reasonableness. Whoever finds them worthless or insecure, has his Bible as it was before to return to.

As to the dislike of them, it is the story of textual criticism over again. The Helvetic Confession formulated a doctrine of sacred Scripture for the Calvinistic churches which implied that we possess an absolutely authentic Greek and Hebrew text. For a century the effort was made to ignore the variations of the manuscripts from the form which had come, almost by accident, into the position of a standard. Beza's great manuscript, antedating by five centuries that from which the so-called "received text" had been taken, was practically suppressed. The Vaticanus, centuries older still, was jealously guarded from publication down to our own day. The pointing out by scholars of variations, as that the oldest manuscripts do not contain the last twelve verses of Mark, or the story of the woman taken in adultery, was bitterly resented. Yet who to-day does not know and rejoice in that very variation, by which, through comparison, we come at a form of text antecedent in many cases to that of any known manuscript?

The history of the higher criticism is exactly analogous. Here the facts to be ascertained are, as we saw, not of the *transmission*, but of the *formation* of the writing, and we are not often so fortunately situated as in the gospels, where we have more than one witness to summon. But the Sermon on the Mount comes to us through two widely variant reports of equal authority. What shall we do in this case? Ignore the differences, deny them, vilify the men who call attention to them, as has been done? Shall we, as is far more common, do our utmost to shut our eyes to them, gloss them over, "harmonize" them, as the expression is? Or shall we be willing to learn from God's word as it is, rather than as it would be convenient for our theories of inspiration to have it? I will assume, for my hearers at least, that they mean to study the Bible with eyes as well as ears wide open, unafraid of what it shall teach them, though every man-made theory of inspiration be overthrown, back to the Nicene Creed, with its single declaration of faith in the Holy Spirit, "who spake by the prophets."

Finally, a word as to the scientific principles on which this method of the higher criticism is based. I have said we should welcome the divergences of our parallel reports for what can be learned from them, inasmuch as we are not in the least alarmed for fear any of our evangelists will be caught in a falsehood. We believe, in fact, that as plain, high-minded, but intensely interested men, they tell the story as they understand it, and with their own selection and emphasis, for their own purpose; to all of which they have a perfect right. Now, this is gospel criticism. The process of research is simply what lawyers call friendly cross-examination. The lawyer cross-questions his own witnesses before the jury. They very likely do not know what he is getting at. But by skilful questioning he manages to draw from mutually independent sources — and the more independent and reciprocally divergent the better, so long as the jury see that they are honest men, each telling the story from his own point of view — a conception of what transpired, that will be identical with the account of no single one of them, and yet better adapted to the jury's comprehension, and nearer the facts, than any. This, I say, is the method of the higher criticism. It is true that there may be *unfriendly* cross-examination, whose object is to make an honest witness appear dishonest, and to obscure rather than elucidate the truth; but this method is as hateful to the true critic as to the devout believer, because it is unscientific. The " special pleader " has no more right in the professor's chair than on the judge's bench.

But comparison of divergent reports is not all, of course; for as you have already reflected, there are portions even of the synoptic writings, like the Book of Acts, where, except in the portions paralleled by the Pauline Epistles, we have practically but *one* witness. What then? Again, ask the lawyer. He does not refrain from friendly cross-examination because he has but one witness. He knows that human testimony invariably consists partly of observation, partly of inference. Let the witness tell his story without interruption in his own way. The more interest he has in the impression his narrative is to make, the stronger will be the emphasis he places on what impresses him, the larger also the element of inference, which in all testimony stands in variable proportion to observed fact. And much of this inference will be honestly stated as fact. But the lawyer knows there may be a different conception of the facts and their bearing. Suppose now, the testimony has been taken by deposition. The witness is absent or dead; there is only his affidavit. Are we no longer able to place a check upon it? Must the disastrous rule be applied: Falsus in uno, falsus in omnibus? Far from it. Surely there is such a thing as consistency or inconsistency with oneself, and with the constant unities of place and time. If you are a lawyer using an affidavit, or a historical critic dealing with the one authority on whom later writers depend, you will certainly sometime be obliged to apply this principle of self-consistency. It is possible to say sometimes, even when we have but a single witness, and to say reasonably, if the right precautions of self-distrust and familiarization with the circumstances are taken, the witness in this particular was mistaken. It is *not* reasonable to say in advance of the experiment, Those whom God has made his witnesses will be excepted from the limitations of all others. Hence, even where we have but a single authority, there is still occasion for historical criticism. Fortunately the cases are rare, in the Sermon on the Mount, where we are reduced to the testimony of a single witness, still more rare in which sayings do not at once vindicate themselves when restored to a more suitable context, while sayings irreconcilable with Jesus' well-established teachings are here at least practically nonexistent.

It may be said, indeed, This method deals only with the human element of the Bible; it does not touch the ultimate mystery of the coming of divine truth into human minds. And this is exactly so. It does not invade the field of metaphysics or doctrinal theology. But what is it to study the Bible? Is it to stand in motionless awe contemplating the inscrutable? Or is it to learn more and more of the invisible by that to which the methods of science can be applied?

By this time you will surely agree that I have not rashly precipitated you unprepared and unwarned into methods of Bible study which some declare untried and dangerous. The method is neither new nor irrational, though prejudice has seemed to demand this brief digression. Let us, then, take up the special problem, asking ourselves, on the basis of all the testimony, logically compared and sifted, What was the discourse, if any, in its fundamental nature and purport, which underlies our so-called Sermon on the Mount?

We begin with what is perhaps a more important question than it seems, the occasion and circumstances, and the persons addressed. On this point we have apparently three witnesses, though really by derivation the three are one. Compare in any gospel harmony the description in Matthew and Luke of the assembled multitudes with that of Mk. 3 : 7–14, and you will see that with minor changes they are word for word the same.* Moreover, it is quite clear that Matthew has here simply borrowed from Mark ; † for, whereas in Mark there is a manifest reason for the assemblage, even from Peræa, Idumea, and Phœnicia, since Jesus' fame as a healer has had time to spread ; in Matthew the assemblage is quite unaccountable, for here the mighty works of Jesus are as yet in the future, save for the sweeping generalization of 4 : 23. Even " his disciples," although addressed according to 5 : 1, were not called until long after.

Luke (6 : 12–19) has made similar use of Mark, his predecessor in the field, though he has not committed the anachronisms of Matthew. He even improves a

---

* See Appendix A (1). The Historical Setting, p. 121.
† Practically all of Mark is taken up in Matthew.

F

little on the order of Mark, putting first Jesus' retirement to "the mountain" and choosing of the twelve; then, "he came down with them and stood on a plain;" then he describes in Mark's language the vast multitude assembled there, who form the background of the audience.*

But this too is a misunderstanding. Has Jesus an appointment with the vast multitudes? How then can he and they so conveniently meet on the plain, when he has been all night on the mountain? Doubtless the "plain" was the real gathering place of the multitude, as Mark and Luke relate; for "*the* mountain" (meaning the highland country back from the populous plain by the lake) is Jesus' regular place of *retirement* from the pressure of the crowds from the cities. Luke probably alters the situation from "mountain" to "plain" for this reason. But what both Matthew and Luke have failed to observe, in borrowing Mark's description

* Appendix A (1), p. 121.

of the crowd, is that in Mark the situation is chosen for a reason just the opposite of that which appeals to them. Jesus in Mark's account is not seeking, but *avoiding*, the multitude. They had come together on the lake-shore in overwhelming numbers, attracted by the fame of Jesus' miracles of healing. But instead of allowing them to throng him and frustrate his real mission by importunities for physical help, Jesus retired to the mountain, eluding the throng, and calling to him only those " whom he himself would," of whom " he appointed twelve that they might be with him, and that he might send them forth to preach." The wisdom of this course is obvious. Now it is at this point that Matthew and Luke both introduce the Sermon on the Mount; rightly, so far as occasion is concerned, wrongly, so far as regards the audience addressed. For the very opening words show that it is really addressed, not to the motley crowd, but to an inner circle of Jesus' followers, who are to be subjects of the kingdom, and through whom the importunate masses are to be reached. But the later evangelists, Matthew and Luke, cannot bear to think that that great multitude below formed no part of the audience; so Matthew makes Jesus take them with him up into the mount, and Luke makes him and the disciples come down again to them into the plain. But the limited character of the circle really addressed, judging by the implications of the discourse itself, forms, as you cannot fail to see, a factor of no small importance for our understanding of it.

The occasion settled, we have next to consider the great contrasts in representation of its content between Luke and Matthew. And first of all the most extensive; the masses of discourse which form part of the Sermon in Matthew, but in Luke are given as uttered on other occasions. We may take two examples. First is the long discourse on earthly and heavenly riches, Mt. 6:

19–34, whose connection with the preceding section on the true worship seems to be merely the refrain, "Thy Father which seeth in secret shall *recompense* thee." *

In Lk. 12 : 13–34 this same discourse on earthly *versus* heavenly riches is given, but in a larger connection.† It follows on a parable of the rich fool, who knew no better wherein life consisteth than when he had increased in wealth to pull down his barns and build greater, and bid his soul enjoy herself. The contrast of the ravens that have "neither storehouse nor barn," yet are fed by God, and of the lilies clothed by Him, is so inimitably apposite that we may be sure this Lucan connection is correct. In fact we may test our synthesis by a comparison of the two parts which in Luke alone appear united. Matthew taken by itself has nothing to explain the philo-

* See Appendix A (8), p. 149.
† See Appendix C, p. 186.

sophical turn of the warning against material anxiety in the words, " Is not *the life* more than the food ? " (Mt. 6 : 35). But in Luke the very question here answered, the question wherein *a man's life* really does consist, whether in provision of food and clothing, or something else, is the question raised at the outset (Lk. 12 : 15). Moreover, it is highly probable that the model for the rich man who seeks only pleasure as the highest good is no other than the Solomon of Ecclesiastes,* a book never employed with approval in the New Testament; and if so, how significant the comparison, " For even *Solomon in all his glory* was not arrayed like one of these ! "

But what led Jesus to this discourse on earthly *versus* heavenly riches ? Luke is explicit. As he was teaching, a man in the crowd appealed to him for a service often rendered by the synagogue

* Compare Eccl. 1 : 12, 16 ; 2 : 1-17.

rabbi,* " Master, bid my brother divide the inheritance with me." Instead of acceding, Jesus refused to be made a judge and divider, and related the parable referred to as a warning against the spirit of covetousness, to show how a man should, and how he should not, " take thought for his life."

It is simply inconceivable that Luke should have invented this admirable historical setting and context. So characteristic a scene can be nothing else but the true occasion of the discourse; the setting created for it by Matthew in the Sermon on the Mount is the reverse of felicitous,† and can only be accounted

---

* Synagogue was town-meeting, and rabbi was lawyer. It was natural that arbitration should be one of the constant and most useful functions of the office. Paul's rebuke of the church in Corinth for resorting to heathen courts, I Cor. 6: 1-7, gains in force and intelligibility from knowledge of the synagogue practice. Jesus' declination of the office of arbitrator is an instance in point of the distinction we have already drawn (p. 29) between his method of teaching and that of the scribes.

† See Appendix A (8), p. 148.

for as an attempt at synthesis (on the theme of "recompense," Mt. 6 : 18) which has resulted in worse disintegration.*

Or take again the Lord's prayer. It is attached in Mt. 6 : 7–15 to the second antithesis illustrating the true acts of worship. The thrice given refrain, " and thy Father which seeth in secret shall recompense thee," concludes the illustration from prayer in v. 6. What follows is in the nature of appended *logia* on prayer. The saying of vv. 14–15 is given again by Matthew himself in its true connection in 18 : 21–35, and is a parallel to Mk. 11 : 25. The Lord's prayer, in simpler form, without the explanatory clauses of Matthew, is given by Luke as part of a great discourse on prayer including, besides this, the com-

---

* The hope of better results from modern than from early synthesis lies in the fact that the modern motive is simply historical and critical, whereas the ancient was as a rule simply practical, either purely mnemonic (*e.g.* Mk. 9 : 33–50) or in the direct interest of edification.

parison of God's giving to that of earthly fathers in Mt. 7 : 7–11 (" Ask and it shall be given you," etc.).* But neither of these formed part of the Sermon on the Mount according to Luke. No; Jesus gave these teachings on prayer, together with the pattern prayer, on a certain occasion when, as he was praying, his disciples came and asked him : " Lord, teach us a prayer, as John the Baptist taught his disciples." † How perverse must be the mind which designates this a fictitious setting ! How blind to what we might learn from the divergences of our witnesses, the man who can do no better than hurry to the rescue with the harmonistic suggestion : " Perhaps Jesus taught the same prayer twice ! "

In a lecture of this kind I cannot, of

* Appendix C, p. 181.

† Again a common practice of the rabbi. Forms of prayer for various occasions were taught the unlearned. The Baptist in this, as in his fastings and his puritanic ideas, was in sympathy with the best type of Pharisaism.

course, go through the entire list of Matthew's additions, pointing out the probable motive and derivation.* Suffice it that the evidence is equally conclusive in several other cases, and so conclusive that those who admit at all this method of study are agreed that we must remove to other contexts many of these appended *logia*, in order to get back to the original discourse. There is no avoiding it. The first step toward real and trustworthy synthesis is along the beaten track of analysis.

But what now of that other great section of the Matthæan discourse, the antithesis of morality and worship in the old law and the new? Were we here to proceed on the simple rule of requiring the consent of both witnesses, the great discourse would be reduced indeed. Here, however, we have not a case of material explicitly related as belonging to another occasion by another witness. As to this, Luke is

* Complete documentary analysis in Appendix A.

simply silent. Moreover, we can account for his silence, and there are even, as we saw,* traces, perhaps faint, but significant, of the former presence of the missing antithesis. We are really applying the same principles as before, when we say of the notion of composition by Matthew, The mind which can attribute a literary and rhetorical unit of such symmetry and beauty to such a compiler is either inept or perverse. Imagine our evangelist framing the exquisite literary balance of the principle Mt. 6 : 1, followed by the three strophes, 2–4, 5–6, 16–18 ; and then wantonly destroying it by inserting the general instructions on prayer, vv. 7–15 ! Or the five antitheses on the new morality, Mt. 5 : 21–48 ; and then throwing in between the first and second the sayings about reconciliation in 5 : 23–26! †
No, we may posit, as nearly all critics now do, a third hand between the evangelist

* *Supra*, p. 17–19.
† Appendix A (5), p. 138.

and the speaker; and we may, with some, make this precanonical author responsible for the exquisite literary finish.* At least he who has so marred it cannot be the same who made it. But artistic as it certainly is, to the degree of almost poetic refinement of expression, I see not why all of even the rhetorical beauty must have been the work of writer rather than of speaker. Why may it not have characterized some of the more studied discourses of the Prophet of Nazareth, rather than the untrained pen of some Galilean publican? We cannot, indeed, imagine Jesus' teaching as *confined* to studied and artificial forms; but neither was it *always* unstudied. Such discourses as that on the Baptist, "What went ye out for to see?"

---

* There are also facts tending to show that the artistic form, while precanonical, is still secondary. *E.g.* the woes against the scribes and Pharisees, in Matthew 23, are *seven* in number, in Luke 2, *three* against the Pharisees followed by *three* against the scribes. Both cannot be original. See Appendix A (6), p.141, and Hawkins's *Horæ Synopticæ*, pp. 131–136.

or that on the sign of Jonah,* can never
have lacked the semi-lyric form of genuine
Hebrew prophecy.†

With the removal of the intrusive elements imported by our first evangelist,
and the restoration of those omitted by
Luke we hold the key to the actual discourse which has come to be our Sermon
on the Mount. Far from being a ram-
bling agglomeration of noble ideas on
half a dozen different subjects, this original nucleus had the characteristic unity
of conception of the parables. In respect
to the section forming the main body of
the Matthæan discourse, the great antithe-

---

* Appendix C, p. 232.

† This striking, perhaps half-unconscious tendency
in the reported discourses of Jesus as in the Prophets
toward a poetic and even lyric structure is well illustrated
in the translations of Moffatt, in his *Historical New
Testament*, 1901. We refer the reader interested in
this special feature of our subject to the works cited
by Mr. Moffatt, p. xx ; as regards the Sermon on the
Mount in particular, to the articles by Professor C. A.
Briggs in the *Expository Times*, viii, pp. 393 f., 452 f.,
493 f.; ix, p. 69 f.

ses on the "righteousness" of the new
kingdom, the *Torah* of Messiah, we must
apply to Luke the same principle we have
just applied to Matthew. This time it is
the Lucan report which decapitates the
most comprehensive discourse of Jesus on
the relation of his doctrine to the past.
The commandment to manifest a spirit of
kindness and serviceableness to all, even
to the unthankful and evil, in imitation of
the divine goodness, which in Lk. 6 : 27–38
stands deprived of its preceding context,
is the counterpart to the righteousness of
the scribes and Pharisees.* This contrast
formed the main subject of the original
discourse. We have only to add at beginning and end the material uttered, on the
undisputed authority of both witnesses, on

---

* It is a further corroboration of our contention as to
the former presence in the Lucan report of the omitted
antitheses, that in the case referred to in our text the
motive appealed to, " Your reward shall be great," etc.
Lk. 6 : 35, *although wanting in the parallel section of
Matthew*, is that, even to phraseology, of the portions
given by Matthew only. See above, p. 38.

this occasion, to have the "sermon" in its original unity and completeness. I mean at the beginning the Beatitudes, which introduce the subject with a congratulation of the hearers on the choice they have made, and at the end the concluding application and parable on the right and wrong use of the principles enunciated. We have seen that this conception of the essential character and purpose of the great discourse, as deliberately enunciating "the Law of Christ," is of no small importance to our understanding of, first, his own conception of his mission ; second, the interpretations subsequently put upon it in the anti-legalistic sense by Paul, in the neo-legalistic sense by James, in the mystical sense by John.

When we come to actual restoration of the discourse there is wide difference in detail between our two authorities ; but in general Luke's account will approve itself to the critic as the simpler and more original, Matthew's as expanded by the attachment here and there of extraneous *logia*. Among these I have mentioned 5 : 23-26, Reconciliation better than Sacrifice, and Let Israel be reconciled with God ere too late.* One need only compare the true context of 25, 26 in Lk. 12 : 54-59 (Interpret the Signs of the Times) † to see that it has really nothing to do with the prohibition of the spirit of anger in the antithesis of Mt. 5 : 21, 22. Similar reasoning applies to the sayings on the Member that causes Stumbling, 5 : 29, 30, attached to the antithesis to the seventh commandment.‡ We find it in its true connection in Mk. 9 : 43-48. The Salt, the Shining Light (5 : 13-16 = Mk. 4 : 21, 22 ; 9 : 49, 50), some of the beatitudes, and a few minor touches are also derived from other contexts.§ Our limitations forbid discussion in detail ; only a guiding principle or two can be indicated as between variant reports.

* Appendix A (5), p. 138.   † Appendix C, p. 246.
‡ Appendix A (6), p. 140.
§ Appendix A (3), p. 130, and Appendix C, p. 258.

Follow the form most closely allied to the principal theme as already established. Reject that which is not germane, injures the sequence of thought, and whose presence can be better accounted for otherwise than by utterance in this connection. When the process of comparison is complete, unless you differ widely from me in your critical judgments, you will have before you as the original discourse that lies behind our reports, the following initial address of Jesus to those whom he had gathered about him as adherents in the effort to give reality to the Kingdom of God. I present it with such aid from historical setting and otherwise as we can gather from all the gospel sources, employing such typographical devices of titles, subtitles, spacing, leading, paragraphing, and alignment to indicate strophic or other rhetorical form, as the modern art of printing suggests. I have also made a somewhat freer translation than that of Authorized or Revised Version, and added

G

reference to parallel reports, where we have them, in the headings, besides a few references of an explanatory character in the margin.   Naturally the report which seems to present the fullest trustworthy statement is made the basis of each paragraph, whether Matthew's, Mark's, or Luke's.   In a few cases the passage from one authority to another requires the supplying of a word. Words thus supplied are enclosed in ( ). Omissions are indicated by * * * with suspended C (1)(2)(3) when the omitted material is given in proper context in Appendix C. Where variant readings have been adopted, a reference is given to Appendix B, for the evidence. The adoption of a different order, or of one evangelist's report in preference to another is similarly indicated by reference to Appendix A.   In typographical arrangement the same plan has been followed as in Appendix C, to which the reader is referred for further explanation and comparison of similar discourses.

Discourse of Jesus on the Higher Law of the Kingdom of God

The Occasion

Mk. 3: 7–15ᵏ = Mt. 4: 24–25; 12: 15–16 =
Lk. 6: 12–19ᴬ⁽¹⁾

Mk. 3 [7] And Jesus with his disciples withdrew to the lake shore; and a great multitude from Galilee followed — [8] and from Judæa and from Jerusalem and from Idumæa and beyond Jordan and about Tyre and Sidon a great multitude, hearing how great things he did came to him.* [9] And he bade his disciples let a boat be in attendance on him ᵃ on account of the crowd, ᵃ Mk. 4: 1. that they might not crush him; [10] for he had healed many, so that they thrust them-

---

* The structure of this sentence, supplementing the "great multitude from Galilee" with a second "great multitude" from remoter parts, is one of the indications referred to in my *Introd.*, p. 206, that the narrative of our Mark employs an older and simpler source, the characteristic "graphic touches of Mark" being ordinarily attached in this supplemental style, as indicated above by the ——. Note again at the end of this paragraph 3: 7–15ᵏ, how the list of apostles' names is attached.

selves upon him to touch him — all that
had scourges.[a]* 11 And the unclean spirits
whenever they beheld him fell down before him and cried out, Thou art the Son
of God.[b] 12 But he commanded them repeatedly not to make him known.

13 Then he goes up into the mountain
(country), and summons those whom he
himself desired and they went away to him.
14 And he appointed the twelve,† that they

---

* The word is peculiar, the only other instances in the
N. T. of its use in this metaphorical sense being in Lk.
7 : 21, and in Mark's story of the woman who was
healed by *touching* Jesus' garment.   Verses 9–12 thus
show their generalizing editorial character ; for in three
consecutive instances we have the anticipation by a proleptic general statement of striking instances, the full account of which follows in the course of the story — the
attendance of the boat (4 : 1), healing by mere contact
from the crowd (5 : 27–29), and recognition by evil
spirits (5 : 6).   In the third case this is already the second instance of such anticipation by the evangelist, he
having made a similar prolepsis in 1 : 24, 34.   In the
second case also the generalization is repeated, the evangelist even going so far in 6 : 56 as to declare that "all
who touched him were made whole."

† The better texts omit "whom he also called
apostles."

might stay with him, and that he might (thereafter) send them out to preach [15] and to have authority to exorcise demons.[a]   [a] 6:7, 12, 13

PART I

THE EXORDIUM: JESUS CONGRATULATES THOSE WHO SEEK THE KINGDOM. CONTRAST OF EARTHLY WITH HEAVENLY GOOD

(1) *Blessedness of those who seek Heavenly Things*

Lk. 6: 20-23 = Mt. 5: 1-12

Lk. 6 [20] And he himself, lifting up his eyes on his disciples, said:

> Blessed are ye poor,
> for yours is the kingdom of God.
> [21] Blessed are ye that hunger, * * *[B]
> for ye shall be filled.
> Blessed are ye that weep, * * *[B]
> for ye shall laugh.

> [22] Blessed are ye when men shall hate you
> * * * [B] and cast out your name as evil * * *.[B]
> Rejoice * * *[B] and leap for joy;

^a Mt. 6: 1, 4, 6, 18.

for, lo, your reward*a* in heaven is
  great ;
after the same manner did they to the
  prophets * * *.*B*

**(2) *Wretchedness of Such as are content with
Earthly Good***

Lk. 6: 24-26

^b Mt. 6: 2, 5, 16.

²⁴ But woe to you that are rich,
    for ye have had your comfort in full.*b*
²⁵ Woe to you that are well filled,
    for ye shall be hungry.
  Woe to you that laugh, * * *^B
    for ye shall mourn.

²⁶ Woe when men shall speak well of you;
    after the same manner did they to the
    false prophets.*

* Reasons for the textual changes indicated are given
in Appendix B (2). Reasons for following the Lucan
as against the Matthæan version as a basis in Appendix A (2). It will be seen that the editorial additions in
the Lucan form are inappreciable in extent, consisting
almost exclusively in the addition of the single word
"now" in verses 21, 22, and 25, to make it clear that
the blessedness of the hungry, sorrowful, hated, is in
their heavenly reward, not in present conditions.

PART II

THE MORAL STANDARD OF THE KINGDOM :
JESUS CONTRASTS THE NEW REQUIRE-
MENT WITH THE OLD

**Thesis: The Divine Commonwealth is
founded on a Law of Absolute Righteousness**

*Jesus shows that the Self-imposed Standard of
the Free Children of the Kingdom is stricter
than the Written Code*

Mt. 5 : 17, 19–20

Mt. 5 [17] Think not that I came to undo
the Law ;
I came not to undo, but to complete.

* * * * *A

[19] Whosoever therefore shall relax
one of these least commandments
and teach men so
shall be called least[a] in the king-   [a] 1 Cor. 15 : 9.
dom of God.
But whoso shall do and teach,
he shall be called great in the
kingdom of God.[A]

²⁰ For I say unto you, Unless your
righteousness abound
 beyond that of the scribes and
 Pharisees
 ye shall not enter into the kingdom of God.

(1) The Royal Law. In Five Antitheses Jesus illustrates the Higher Principle of Duty to Man, contrasting it with the Current Rules of Conduct

Mt. 5: 21–48 mostly. Fragments in Luke

*First Antithesis : He forbids the Spirit of Hatred
as against Prohibition of Murder and Libel*

Mt. 5: 21–22

Mt. 5 ²¹ Ye have heard that it was said to
 the ancients,
 Thou shalt not kill, and whosoever killeth
 he shall be amenable to judgment.
²² But I say unto you,
 Whosoever is angry with his
 brother
 shall be amenable to judgment.

(Moreover it was said),[B(3)] *
Whosoever shall call his brother
    Scoundrel
shall be amenable to the court.
[23] But I say unto you,
Whosoever calleth him Simpleton
shall be amenable to the hell of
    fire. †

*Second Antithesis : Jesus forbids the Impure
Thought as against the Adulterous Deed*

Mt. 5 : 27–28, 31–32[A(6)] = Lk. 16 : 18

Mt. 5 [27] Ye have heard that it was said,
    Thou shalt not commit adultery.
[28] But I say unto you,
    Every one that looketh on a
      woman lustfully
    hath already committed adultery
      with her in his heart.

* For the conjectural emendation of text see Appendix B (3) and Note by J. P. Peters, D.D., in *Journ. of Bib. Lit.*, 1892, i. p. 131.

† The sense is, the new standard is absolute. The malicious thought, the opprobrious epithet, even if not legally actionable, will suffice to cast into the outer darkness, the place where offal was destroyed. Jewish law was exceptionally severe against slander and libel. The new law surpasses even this.

³¹ Moreover it was said,
> Whoso would put away his wife
> must give her a certificate of
> divorce.*

³² But I say unto you,
> Every one that putteth away his
> wife   *   *   * ^{B(4)} committeth
> adultery ^a;
> and whoso marrieth her that was
> divorced committeth adultery.

^a Mk. 10: 11–12; Lk. 16: 18.

*Third Antithesis : Jesus forbids Untruthfulness
as against the Prohibition of Perjury*

Mt. 5: 33–37

Mt. 5 ³³ Again ye have heard that it was
> said to the ancients,
> Forswear not thyself,
> but perform thine oaths to the
> Lord.

³⁴ But I say unto you
> Swear not at all:
> neither by heaven, for it is God's
> throne;

³⁵ nor by earth, for it is his foot-
> stool;

* A humane restriction of the Mosaic law upon the
unlimited right of repudiation allowed to the husband in
the days when woman had been a chattel only.

nor by Jerusalem, for it is the
city of the great King;

36 neither by thy head, for thou
canst not make one hair white
or black.*

37 *a* But let your yea be yea, and
your nay nay,B(5)

   a Jas. 5:12.

what exceedeth this is from the
Evil One.†

*Fourth Antithesis: Jesus forbids Ill-treatment
of Any Man, as against the Limitation of
Retaliation*

Mt. 5:38–42; 7:12 = Lk. 6:29–31

Mt. 5 38 Ye have heard that it was said,
An eye (only) for an eye, and a
tooth (only) ‡ for a tooth.

39 But I say unto you,
Resist not the violent.

* Mt. 23:16–22 shows how scribal casuists had
yielded to the besetting sin of their kind, inventing
forms of oaths for evading their obligation. A simple
yes or no must suffice in the kingdom.

† That is, proceeds from the intent to deceive or the
assumption of its possibility. Both are inadmissible sup-
positions in the divine commonwealth.

‡ Another humane limitation imposed by the Mosaic
law on the wild blood revenge of the primitive Bedouin;
cf. Gen. 4:23–24.

Lk. 6 [29] To him that smiteth thee on the
cheek
offer also the other.

Mt. 5 [40] And if any would sue thee and
take thy cloak *
let him have the tunic as well.
[41] And whoso would impress thee
for one mile,
go with him two.
Give to him that asketh,
and from him that would borrow
turn not away.

7 [12] So whatsoever ye would that
men should do unto you,
do even so unto them * * *.[B(6)]

*Fifth Antithesis: Jesus imposes an Unlimited
and Universal as against a Limited Obligation of Kindness*

Mt. 5: 43-48 = Lk. 6: 27-28, 32-36

Mt. 5 [43] Ye have heard that it was said
Love thy neighbor and hate †
thine enemy,

---

* That is, show himself a merciless creditor.   Mosaic
law forbade taking the cloak over night, Ex. 22: 26–27;
Deut. 24: 10–13.

† A Semitic method of emphasizing a distinction

⁴⁴ But I say unto you,
    Love your enemies,
    and pray for them that persecute
        you ;
⁴⁵ that ye may be sons of your
        Father in heaven.
    For he maketh his sun to rise
        on both wicked and good,
    and the rain to fall on just and
        unjust.

⁴⁶ For if ye love them that love
        you, what credit[a] have ye ?
    Do not the very tax-gatherers
        the same ?

[a] 5: 12; 6: 2, 5, 16; Lk. 6: 35.

(cf. Mt. 10: 37 = Lk. 14: 26). The O. T. does not, of course, affirmatively inculcate hatred, even to enemies, but simply assumes, and occasionally exemplifies it, as in the imprecatory psalms ; this being involved in the limitation of its requirement of good-will to the "neighbor" (Lev. 19: 18). The present passage shows that Jesus is not ignorant of the real meaning of the commandment Lev. 19: 18, although he employs it (Mt. 22: 39), and even — in the *haggadic* sense — interprets and applies it (Lk. 10: 27–37) in a sense transcending its original intent. In other words, he is perfectly conscious that he is imposing a higher standard than that of the *Torah*.

⁴⁷ And if ye say 'God be with
you ' * to your brethren only,
what credit have ye ?

Do not the very Gentiles the
same ?

Lk. 6 ³⁵ But love your enemies,
and do good and lend without
hope of return
and your reward shall be great,ᵃ
and ye shall be sons of the
Highest ;
for he is kind even to the unthankful and the wicked.

Mt. 5 ⁴⁸ Ye therefore shall be complete in
goodness †
as your Father in heaven is
complete.ᴮ⁽⁷⁾

ᵃ Mt. 5 : 12,
46, 47 ; 6 : 2,
5, 16.

* Literally, " give greeting." But the Jewish greeting was a sacred blessing which, it was thought, would
be profaned if invoked on the heathen or infidel. Hence
the prohibition in 2 Jn. 10–11, which shows more of
the spirit rebuked by Jesus in Mk. 9 : 38 than that of the
present passage. Hence also the general directions in
Mt. 10 : 12–13 ; Lk. 10 : 4. We translate " say 'God be
with you ' " to bring out the correspondence with v. 44,
" Pray for them that persecute you."

† Τέλειος is doubtless employed here by the evangelist
precisely as in 19 : 21, of the ultimate stage of righteous-

(2) The Spiritual Worship. In Three Further Antitheses Jesus illustrates the Higher Principle of Duty to God, contrasting it with Current Types of Piety

Mt. 6: 1–6, 16–18

The Principle : Worship must be in Spirit and Truth

Mt. 6: 1

Mt. 6 [1] Take heed to your acts of piety
that ye do them not before men
to be seen of them,
Otherwise ye have no reward[a]
with your Father in heaven.

[a] 5: 12, 46; Lk. 6: 35.

First Illustrative Antithesis : Almsgiving

Mt. 6: 2–4

Mt. 6 [2] Thus when thou art giving alms,
make not a flourish of trumpets *
as do the hypocrites

ness. Luke renders *ad sensum* οἰκτίρμονες, " compassionate " ; which is correct in meaning but fails to bring out the contrast intended with the limited obligation assumed in the casuistry of the scribes and Pharisees. Compare Jesus' teaching on the limit of forgiveness, Mt. 18: 21–22.

* Probably only a metaphor. Actual trumpet blowing is improbable. Even an allusion to the trumpet-

in the synagogues and on the
streets

that they may be honored by
men.

Of a truth I say unto you,

They have their reward*a* in full.*

a Mt. 5 : 12,
46; Lk. 6 : 35.

3 But thou, when thou art giving
alms,

let not thy left hand know what
thy right is doing,†

4 that thine almsgiving may be in
secret;

And thy Father which seeth in
secret

shall recompense thee.‡

shaped bronze orifices of the temple contribution boxes,
which could doubtless be "sounded" with a good-sized
coin, is at the best a precarious supposition.

* On the sense of ἀπέχεσθαι, the technical term employed in receipts in the contemporary Greek papyri to
signify discharge of the obligation, see Deissmann, *Bible
Studies*, 1900, *s.v.* Deissmann renders, "They may give
their receipt in full."

† Perhaps an allusion to the Pharisees' ostentatious
passing of the coin from one hand to the other, that bystanders may not fail to be impressed.

‡ The principle, "He that giveth to the poor lendeth
to the Lord," is not in dispute. Granting that almsgiving
is an act of piety deserving reward, and so a way to

Second Antithesis : Prayer

Mt. 6 : 5–6

Mt. 6 ⁵ And when ye are praying
be not like the hypocrites ;
for they love to stand and pray
in the synagogues
and on the corners of the streets,*
that they may be seen of men.
Of a truth I say unto you,
They have their reward in full.
⁶ But thou, when thou prayest,
enter into the inner room
and shut the door,
and pray in secret to thy Father;
and thy Father, which seeth in
secret,
shall recompense thee.

lay up treasure in heaven (cf. Lk. 16: 1–9), Jesus points
out that it cannot *both* be laid up in heaven and enjoyed
(in the shape of honor from men) on earth. This is simply an illustration of the fallacy that the play-actors' worship (ἡ τοῦ ὑποκριτοῦ) puts God under some obligation.
Such worship cannot, for it is not really directed to him,
but to the bystanders. Jesus is not committed, however,
by the illustration, to the doctrine that God can be made
debtor to a man by his almsgiving (cf. Lk. 17: 10).

* Overtaken midway by the hour of prayer (9 A.M.,
or 3 P.M.).

H

Third Antithesis: Fasting

Mt. 6: 16–18

Mt. 6 ¹⁶ And when ye are fasting,
be not like the hypocrites
wry-faced ;
for they disfigure their faces
that they may figure* as fasting
before men.
Of a truth I say unto you,
They have their reward in full.
¹⁷ But thou, when thou art fasting,
Anoint thy head and wash thy
face,
¹⁸ that thou appear not as a faster
unto men,
but unto thy Father [that is in
secret ?].[B(8)]
And thy Father [that seeth in
secret][B(8)]
shall recompense thee.†

---

*'Αφανίζουσιν ὅπως φανῶσιν, a word-play, if not acci-
dental.

† We may notice that the antitheses of the true worship conclude with a reference to future recompense, as
did the exordium (Lk. 6: 22) and the antitheses of the
true ethics (Lk. 6: 35). See above, pp. 86 and 94.

PART III

APPLICATION OF THE NEW LAW. JESUS
SHOWS HOW TO USE, AND HOW NOT TO
USE ITS STANDARD

First Principle

Not for Censoriousness, but Self-correction

Mt. 7 : 1–5 = Lk. 6 : 37ᵃ, 38ᵇ, 41–42

Mt. 7 ¹ Judge not, that ye be not judged ;
² for with what judgment ye judge
ye shall be judged
[and with what measure ye measure out, it shall be measured
back to you ?].ᴬ⁽⁹⁾

³ But why regardest thou the splin-
ter in thy brother's eye
but considerest not the beam in
thine own eye ?
⁴ Or how wilt thou say to thy
brother,
let me remove the splinter from
thine eye,
and, lo, there is a beam in thine
own eye ?

⁵ Hypocrite, remove first the beam
from thine own eye

> and then shalt thou see clearly to remove the splinter from thy brother's eye.

Second Principle

Reform must be from Within

Mt. 7 : 18 ; 12 : 33, 35 = Lk. 6 : 43, 45

Mt. 7 ¹⁸ A good tree cannot bear bad
bad fruit,
nor a rotten tree produce good
fruit.

12 ³³ Either make the tree good and
its fruit good,
or make the tree rotten and its
fruit rotten.

*　　　*　　　*　　　*　　　* A(10)

³⁵ The good man from his good store
bringeth forth good things,
and the evil man from his evil
store bringeth forth evil things.

Third Principle

Deeds, not Words demanded

Lk. 6 : 46–49 = Mt. 7 : 21–27

Thesis　　Lk. 6 ⁴⁶ And why call ye me Lord,
Lord, and do not the
things which I say?

Parable [47] Every one that heareth my words
and doeth them,

shall be likened to a wise man,

Mt. 7 [24 b] that built his house upon a
rock.[B(9)]

[48] The rains poured down, the
floods came,

the winds blew and beat upon
that house ;

and it fell not,

Mt. 7 [25 b] for it was founded on the rock.

[26] And every one that heareth my
words

and doeth them not,

shall be likened to a foolish man,

that built his house upon the
sand.[B(9)]

[27] The rain poured down, the floods
came,

the winds blew and beat upon
that house ;

and it fell

and the fall thereof was great.*

* O. Holtzmann (*Leben Jesu*, p. 77) points out that
with Jesus metaphors from the builder's trade are specially frequent, confirming the view that τέκτων in Mk.
6: 3 should be rendered " builder."

The Colophon

Mk. 1 : 22 = Mt. 7 : 28 = Lk. 7 : 1[a]

Mt. 7 [28] And it came to pass when Jesus had finished these sayings, the crowds were amazed at his teaching ; [29] for his way of teaching them was as of one that has authority, and not as their scribes.

An Appended Incident

Healing of the Centurion's Servant

Lk. 7 : 1[b]–10 = Mt. 8 : 5–10, 13 = Jn. 4 : 46[b]–54

Lk. 7 [1] And he entered into Capernaum. [2] And a certain centurion had a slave that was dear to him, who was sick and at the point of death.   [3] And when he heard about Jesus he sent elders of the Jews unto him,[a] asking him to come and heal his slave.   [4] And these came to Jesus and besought him earnestly, [5] saying that the man was worthy[b] that he should do this for him ; for he loveth our nation, and himself built the synagogue for us.   [6] And Jesus went with them.   But when he was already

[a] Acts 10 : 5.

[b] Acts 10 : 2.

not far from the house, the centurion sent friends[a] to say to him, My lord, take no trouble; for I am not of dignity enough that thou shouldst enter beneath my roof. 7 For this reason also I did not deem myself worthy to come to thee (in person); but give direction by a word and my servant shall be healed.   8 For I too am a man ranked under authority, having soldiers under me, and I say to one, Go, and he goeth, and to another, Come, and he cometh, and to my slave, Do this, and he doeth it. 9 And when Jesus heard this he marvelled at him, and turned and said to the crowd that followed him : I tell you I have not seen so great faith not even in Israel.

10 Now when the messengers had returned home they found the slave convalescent.

Such in context and content is the Sermon on the Mount after application of the methods of the higher criticism, the processes which you may have heard described

[a] Acts 10 : 25 β text.

— often with large expenditure of wit at
the expense of a little body of indefatigable
scholars—as "cutting the Bible to pieces."
I must leave you to judge whether the ac-
cusations are deserved. One thing is certain. Whatever external and more or less
artificial unity of connection to which we
have grown accustomed is broken up, no
thoughtful person can deny that unity of
thought and logical connection characterize
the discourse as thus conjecturally restored
in far higher degree than the Matthæan
composite, as we must now consider it. In
other words, the process decried as a cutting to pieces is one which tends, in all
that lies behind the mere dead letter, to
unity and order, a process which results
not in a chaotic mass of *disjecta membra*,
but in organic unities of logical sequence
and literary beauty. Some accustomed
portions of the pile are gone indeed. We
miss the logical and literary excrescences.
But what has become of them? Were they
"cast as rubbish to the void"? On the

contrary, restored to their appropriate context, they have no longer even the appearance of excrescences which was put upon them only by displacement. Of the value of these methods in the given instance you must judge by the results. If both analysis and synthesis produce a gain in perspicacity and order, if in such salient examples as the discourse on the True Content of Life or Earthly *versus* Heavenly Riches, the Discourse on Prayer, and the Warning to Israel to be Reconciled ere too late with her great Adversary, not only the Sermon on the Mount is the gainer by the removal, but the section removed by its new setting, then the method is justified both by its logic and its results. We shall be warranted in seeking to apply it further.

But the result in the specific instance of the great discourse on the Higher Righteousness is what now concerns us. Grant that we have succeeded in establishing a connected logical unity and in exhibiting in outline its principal substance, and it will be impossible, I think, to deny that our first evangelist is right in his apparent design to depict Jesus in the attitude of a second Moses, a title expressly given him by the primeval Jewish church. Not that Jesus put himself forward as such a law-giver, even in the inner circle of his disciples. Quite the contrary. But that he was fully conscious that nothing would fully meet their need, which did not wholly replace for them that institution which in the heart of every true Jew was dominant over every other consideration, religious or secular — the Law, the *Torah* divinely revealed to Moses, Israel's charter as the People of God. To be a People of God in very truth, and as he would have them, Jesus knew that the great cry and expectation of his people for a new law must be met. And in form he gave it to them. In form even the briefer utterance which we take to be the original discourse is a new *Torah*. Jesus assumed personally the authority not indeed to enact, but to make known the absolute divine law, as it must needs be under the ideal conditions of the kingdom he proclaimed. The antitheses of old and new, past and future requirement, cannot be eliminated, and will bear no other interpretation. In form the very watchword of legalism is adopted — "recompense." "Great is your reward in heaven," "your reward shall be great," "else ye have no reward," "He that seeth in secret shall reward thee." It seems to echo everywhere the Pharisaic idea, "What shall I do that I may have a claim on eternal life?" In form it is as completely neo-legalistic as the Matthæan answer to this question. In reality there is just as much and just as little of literalness in the intention of the answer as in the reply, "Go, sell all that thou hast and give to the poor, and thou shalt have treasure in heaven, and come, follow me to martyrdom." The expectation of the legalist is met to the ear, but broken to the hope. Jesus' paradox seems to promise that a little further effort along the line of the righteousness of scribe and Pharisee will gain the long coveted reward. In reality the new requirement is so exorbitant that all mere mercenary righteousness collapses before it and "turns away sorrowful." Mere hope of heavenly recompenses cannot face such requirements as forbid not only the act of hate or lust, but the slightest unkind word or impure thought, and command the turning of the other cheek in place of retaliation. Even a Saul of Tarsus found the struggle hopeless when the law demanded, "Thou shalt not *desire*." * When, therefore, the New Law culminates in the positive requirement of unlimited love and service even to the unthankful and evil, because such is the righteousness exercised by God, and promises on this condition, "Your reward shall be great — ye

---

* Rom. 7 : 7. Saul's Bible was Greek, and the Greek Οὐκ ἐπιθυμήσεις conveys this sense. Evil desire, ἐπιθυμία, is to Paul the essence of sin.

shall be children of the Highest," it is *not* expected that the Pharisaic spirit will be attracted, but rather supremely disappointed. In such rare atmosphere it can no longer sustain itself. He who obeys the law in mere hope of reward must turn away a wiser if a sadder man.

And if in all the succeeding section on the God-ward duties, almsgiving, prayer, fasting, the refrain, "Thy Father shall reward thee," still recurs, such (to the legalist) vague assurance in place of the detailed and specific promises extracted by the rabbis from Scripture will have seemed like mockery after what precedes.

What then is the fundamental nature of this discourse, as the closest critical scrutiny reveals it ? In a single word it is not legislative, as our first evangelist seems to regard it, but prophetic. It does not enact, but interprets. It does not lay down rules, but opens up principles. It was indeed from the standpoint of the historian of Jesus' life and teaching a disastrous, almost incredible mutilation to leave out, as our third evangelist has done, all the negative side of the teaching, and give nothing but the commandment of ministering love toward all. We can scarcely understand that the five great interpretative antitheses of the new law of conduct toward men *versus* the old, and the three corresponding antitheses on duty toward God, could have been dropped in one form of even the oral tradition; still less that an evangelist, anxious to " set forth in order a declaration " of the full content of Christian tradition, after "accurately tracing it up to the very first," should have deliberately cancelled such invaluable material. And yet our third evangelist, by thus concentrating upon the simple affirmation of the law of love, shows that in real insight into the Speaker's purpose he surpasses the author of the fuller report. Matthew, as we have seen, is quite absorbed in the relation of the new *Torah* to the old. So much so that he fails to appreciate that his material is not really a series of new enactments, but in reality, just as Luke perceives, a simple application to the situation of that one principle which Jesus elsewhere enunciates more briefly; and not then as enacting something new, but as explaining the old. A certain scribe came unto him with one of the debated questions of the day: Rabbi, which is the great commandment of the Law? Jesus went further than the great Hillel had gone in the saying, "What thou wouldest not that others should do unto thee, do not unto them; this is the whole Law, the rest is commentary." Jesus replied: "Thou shalt love the Lord thy God with all thy heart, and with all thy soul, and with all thy mind. This is the first and great commandment. And the second is like unto it, Thou shalt love thy neighbor as thyself. On these two commandments hang all the Law and the Prophets." *

* Mt. 22: 35–40.

As our Johannine interpreter has shown,* even these two are one.

What now is our great discourse on the new *Torah* but an expansion of this one "new commandment" in its two divisions, and application of it to the question, How shall the Law be renewed in the Kingdom of Messiah? The five antitheses of ethics are not so many new enactments in place of the old. They are not the substitution of one new and broader rule of conduct toward men, in place of many. They are not rules at all. They are illustrations of the one *principle* which Jesus saw in "all the Law and the Prophets," and saw as well in all nature and history, that the divine calling is to ministering love and service — that, and that alone. The three antitheses of religion are not so many new enactments in place of the Mosaic ceremonial. They are not even the substitu-

* Jn. 2:5–15; 3:10–18; 4:16–21; 5:1–3; Jn. 15: 9–14, 17.

tion of one universal rule of worship in spirit and in truth for innumerable forms. They are not rules. They *illustrate*, in the particular problem, What is the relation of worship in the kingdom of God to that now current ? — the one *principle* that the divine calling to ministering love and service is a calling of man into the fellowship of his own nature, a relation of sonship and fatherhood.

This, then, is the real and fundamental significance of the great discourse on the New Law of Christ. Taken as a whole it exhibits the mystical sense of its opening paradox, " I came not to destroy, but to fulfil." In Pauline language, " Christ is the end of the Law unto righteousness for every one that believeth ; " because all the Law is fulfilled in this one word, " Thou shalt love thy neighbor as thyself," and the new " Law of Christ," that we " bear one another's burdens," is not a law, but an animating spirit. Thus the purpose of the Law is achieved, not indeed

I

by its hopes of reward and threats of penalty, but by the gift of a new divine disposition from Him who alone is "good"; and being achieved, the Law is done away.

In the mind of the great Teacher accordingly the form of a New Law in which he casts his teaching is a form only. The legalistic conception is as foreign to it as when Paul himself employs the term "the law of Christ." His hearers' minds are as completely fettered by the current legalism as that of the young ruler, prototype of Saul, whom he "looked upon and loved." And Jesus takes their point of view. Not indeed wholly as a matter of condescension; for, *as a form*, it is as natural to him as to them. But his deeper religious sense, the mysticism of his God-consciousness, triumphs over it. In the very adoption of this legal form for his demand of righteousness,* he shows them their need

* On this point, see Beyschlag, *op. cit.*, Vol. I. ch. 5, § 1.

of a higher, because when they have done all, they will still have no claim to eternal life. The most they can say on the basis of merit will be : "We are unprofitable servants. We have done that which it was our duty to do."

Long, indeed, was it before the church could apprehend this higher point of view. Even the polemic anti-legalism of Paul could not lift the dead weight of centuries of training under the conception of "moral government." We trace the reactionary tendency in the additions of the compiler of the Sermon on the Mount, evidenced by the variant report of Luke and by inherent inconsistency with the context, in further additions of scribes of mediæval times, evidenced by the variation of manuscripts, finally in the unconscious additions of modern interpreters, all in the same direction, all assuming that after all Jesus, in this case, was a casuist and not a preacher ; a legislator, not a herald of the glad tidings ; that he taught rules of conduct rather than principles of religion.

Take as examples of that neo-legalistic coloration which precedes the formation of our first gospel, the scrupulous qualifications attached in the Matthæan form of the Beatitudes, guarding the terms on which the blessings may be had, as though the Speaker had been too liberal with his offer of the divine bounty for a general audience; the clause in v. 16, which explains the "light" as "good works"; above all, the insertion of 5 : 18 with its insistence on the minutiæ of the *letter* of the Law in the midst of a context which aims to free from the letter and exalt the spirit.

As examples of the continuation of the same process by mediæval scribes take the addition from Ps. 37 : 11 to the Beatitudes, the proviso in Mt. 5 : 11 that the evil speaking endured must be "false" to deserve reward, and the addition "without a cause" to the prohibition of anger in 5 : 22.

Even so noble and free a spirit as Tolstoi in modern times cannot free himself from the misconception of Jesus as a casuist in his interpretation of the doctrine of non-resistance. But more often literalism is applied to the antithesis of goodness as the cure for wrong rather than retaliation, sometimes involving disparagement of the great Teacher, as if he had really attempted to sit in Moses' seat, and had shown his unfitness for practical legislation. Yet an immense majority of laymen and ecclesiastics, even among Protestants, sin just as egregiously against the real meaning of Jesus, when they attempt to formulate an ecclesiastical law of divorce on the basis of Mt. 5 : 32. It is true that they have here the bad example of the evangelist, who by inserting the exception " save on account of fornication " here and in Mt. 19 : 9 perverts the sense, and contradicts every other reference of the New Testament *; but in spite of this textual

* Appendix B (4), p. 177.

corruption the whole spirit of the passage, the Sermon on the Mount as a whole, and Jesus' teaching on other occasions should have taught us that Jesus was not enacting a divorce law, but preaching, like the prophet Malachi, "The Lord hateth putting away." It is chosen to serve as a second illustration in the antithesis on purity of thought *versus* action, because of the base motive which then as now was in most cases directly or indirectly the cause of "putting away." The word of Jesus leaves the Christian statesman absolutely untrammelled to legislate on this subject simply and solely for the highest interests of the family, the state, and social order. If he be truly loyal to the teaching of Christ he will legislate, whether stringently or loosely, as he deems best for these interests, because they are also the interests of the Kingdom of God.

In conclusion, I can but urge you to a study of the great discourse itself. Understand Jesus by his own words read to the utmost in their original setting and connection. Who is Paul, and who is Apollos, who is Matthew, or Luke, or John, but ministers through whom we believe? Understand Jesus as a prophet, a preacher, a herald of glad tidings, and all these first to his own times. And as you come more and more fully to understand him thus, more and more fully will you find him for all time and times, the Way, the Truth, and the Life.

APPENDIX A

ANALYTICAL NOTES

(1) *The Historical Setting*

Mk. 3: 7–12 = Mt. 12: 15, 16; 4: 24, 25 =
Lk. 6: 17–19

In Mark, our earliest gospel, the description
of the importunate multitudes flocking to Jesus
as the result of his spreading fame as a healer
introduces an important section of the biography.
The preceding section, 2 : 1–3 : 6, had illustrated
how Jesus' independent ways brought him into
more and more serious collision with the
authorities, culminating in the plot against his
life, 3 : 6. The evangelist returns now to the
point reached at the close of the first chapter,
where the disobedience of those he healed to
his injunctions of silence had resulted in serious
injury to his real work of evangelization, " so
that he was no longer able openly to enter a
city, but was without in desert places, and they
came to him from every quarter." In 3 : 7–

6 : 12 the evangelist explains how Jesus met the problem (*a*) by the selection and training of a group of disciples, 3 : 13–35, (*b*) by the teaching in parables, 4 : 1–34.   The series of incidents in 4 : 35–5 : 43 are illustrative of 3 : 14, 15, how Jesus trained the Twelve to " go forth and preach " and to " have power over demons." The episode of 3 : 19ᵇ–35 is introduced to show how Jesus gave his disciples the place of his earthly kin, and is itself forced apart by the insertion of the story of the unforgivable blasphemy of the scribes from Jerusalem, 3 : 22–30, by way of contrast with the pardonable fault of Jesus' mother and brethren.*   The episode of Jesus' rejection in Nazareth, 6 : 1–6, stands where it does as a kind of colophon to the story of Jesus' personal preaching.   " His own received him not."

---

* But a totally independent version of this saying and its occasion (My mother and brethren are " they that hear the word of God and keep it ") is given in Lk. 11 : 27–28 which coincides with Mark's in the representation that it was uttered on the day of the great collision with " the scribes from Jerusalem " (vv. 15–22). This would indicate actual historical coincidence and not merely collocation for didactic purposes.

The general description, Mk. 3 : 7–12, thus constitutes the introduction to that whole section of the gospel which ends with the Mission of the Twelve, 6 : 7–12. It is natural therefore that the evangelist should anticipate here some of the illustrative special traits he subsequently relates in their specific connection. Striking examples of such prolepsis appear (*a*) in v. 9, where the utilization of the boat as an extemporized pulpit is anticipated from 4 : 1, (*b*) in v. 10, where the endeavor of those who had " scourges " (μάστιγας, as in 5 : 29, 34) to touch him is anticipated from 5 : 27, and (*c*) in v. 11, which generalizes the specific instances subsequently related in 5 : 6. These instances clearly establish the character and purpose of Mk. 3 : 7–12, at the same time justifying the primeval tradition as to the order of Mark generally as representing rather the exigencies of didactic method (πρὸς τὴν χρείαν) than chronological order (οὐ μέντοι τάξει).*

---

* Modern criticism is so much impressed with the *relatively* original and historical order of Mark, as compared with our other gospels, as to pay altogether too little attention to this real characteristic.

No good critic who reads side by side Mk. 3 : 7–12 and Lk. 6 : 17–19 will deny the dependence of Luke, so that demonstration would here be a waste of words.

The matter is somewhat different in Matthew, because in this gospel two parts are made of the description. Mk. 3 : 7, 10ᵃ, 12 are utilized in Mt. 12 : 15–21 to introduce in vv. 22–50 that which next follows in Mark, the blasphemy of the scribes from Jerusalem *vs.* the opposition of Jesus' mother and brethren. The appointment and list of the Twelve (Mk. 3 : 13–19) drops out because already given from the *Logia* source (Mt. 10 : 1–4). The rest (Mk. 3 : 8, 10, 11), omitting the proleptic special features, is utilized in Mt. 4 : 24, 25 for the same purpose as in Luke. This coincidence, as Wendt * remarks, may be accounted for on the supposition that in the *Logia* a similar situation was given for the discourse,† in view of the fact that both evangelists, in spite of their representation of Jesus as surrounded by vast multitudes, begin by saying that he addressed

* *Lehre Jesu*, Vol. I. p. 53.
† See, however, p. 65.

his " disciples." And such would seem to be the nature of the discourse itself, though by μαθηταί it certainly meant more than the Twelve alone.

(2) *The Beatitudes*

Mt. 5: 1–12 = Lk. 6: 20–24, and Woes, Lk. 6: 24–26

On the question whether Luke or Matthew, as between the two widely discrepant representations of the introductory portion of the address, represents greater originality, the judgment of Holtzmann * and Wendt † is certainly correct. As Wendt has shown, the supposed Ebionism of the Lucan source is not present. Not the *conditions of admission* to the kingdom of God are laid down, else even Matthew, with all its endeavor to remove their apparently unethical character, will still have left in 5 : 4 and 11 traits obnoxious to moral feeling, but its subjects are congratulated on the *superiority* of its blessings to those of this world. The contrast is between external and spiritual good, and is exactly in line with the antitheses of the new and old, external *vs.* spiritual morality, which Luke nevertheless does not contain. It is still more

* *Synopt. Evang.*, p. 76 f. † *Op. cit.*, p. 53.

distinctly in line with the contrast of worship:
the Pharisee, who worships to be seen of men,
and "has his reward," and the son of the Kingdom whose reward is from "thy Father that
seeth in secret." In the lecture attention is
called to the identity even in phraseology.

It is not here Matthew but *Luke* who writes
6 : 23, "Rejoice for great is *your reward* in
heaven;" 24, "Woe to you rich, for *ye have
received to the full* (ἀπέχετε) your consolation;"
35, "And *your reward* shall be great."

The contrasting "woes" are also certainly
original, not merely because of the thought and
phraseology, as already suggested, but because
the balance of the discourse in all its other parts
between old and new, outward and inward, material and spiritual, requires it.

Thirdly, Luke is correct in employing the
second person, to which even Matthew passes
over in 11 and 12. It does not follow because
no rich men were presumably present, that Jesus
did not apostrophize them, as in Lk. 6 : 24; for
in Lk. 10 : 13; 13 : 34, 35 we have similar
instances, and in Jas. 5 : 1–6 a still closer parallel. The change to the third person is part of

a process of generalization of the teaching in Matthew of which we have now to speak.

The secondary character of the Matthæan form is apparent (*a*) in the numerical arrangement apparent throughout this gospel; * (*b*) in the addition of explanatory clauses; (*c*) in the toning down of strong rhetorical figures toward the commonplaces of catechetic instruction.

Under (*a*) we notice here that we have just *seven* beatitudes, corresponding to the *seven* (originally *five*) clauses of the Lord's Prayer, the *seven* parables of ch. 13, and the *seven* woes of ch. 23; for v. 5, whose position varies in the β text, is a mere scribal gloss, a marginal addition from Ps. 37:11, which has crept in after v. 3 in some manuscripts, after v. 4. in others. This threefold recurrence of groups of seven is, therefore, doubtless the work of the compiler (Matthew[iii]), especially as he makes up in chapters 8-9 a similar group of *ten* miracles.

(*b*) The addition of the clauses τῷ πνεύματι (v. 3), καὶ διψῶντες τὴν δικαιοσύνην (v. 6), ψευδόμενοι (v. 11), τοὺς πρὸ ὑμῶν (v. 12) tends

---

* See Hawkins, *Horæ Synopticæ*, p. 132, and Holtzmann, *Handkommentar*, p. 11. But cf. *infra*, p. 169.

to adjust the meaning to the common view or
to remove difficulties. We cannot suppose that
though original, they were omitted by Luke.
Their editorial insertion by Matthew is perfectly
comprehensible.

(*c*) The general result of the changes from
second to third person, introduction of new
beatitudes (vv. 7, 9, 10) commending all sorts
of virtues, explanatory additions to guard against
a non-ethical interpretation, tends to generalize
the teaching adapting the discourse to service as
a compendium of rules of right living. This
effaces the strong lines of the original thought,
as determined by the constant contrasts which
follow. It is characteristic of this evangelist
(Matthew[iii]) that he is considerate of ortho-
doxy, conforming inexact quotations to the letter
of scripture (Mt. 13 : 14–15, cf. Mk. 4 : 12 ;
19 : 18–19, cf. Mk. 10 : 19), and changing
Mark's plain $\beta a\sigma\iota\lambda\epsilon\iota a$ $\tau o\hat{v}$ $\theta\epsilon o\hat{v}$ to the more rev-
erent (?) circumlocution $\beta a\sigma\iota\lambda\epsilon\iota a$ $\tau\hat{\omega}\nu$ $o\vec{v}\rho a\nu\hat{\omega}\nu$.
While it is no unreasonable supposition of O.
Holtzmann's that Jesus in this respect may have
followed the usage of his countrymen (cf. Lk.
15 : 21), Matthew[iii]'s practice in the sections he

borrows from Mark makes it reasonable to regard βασιλεία τῶν οὐρανῶν as secondary everywhere.

The result is for us an unavoidable adoption of the Lucan form (three beatitudes and an explanatory expansion, vv. 22–23, followed by three woes in antithetic form) as the more original. The exordium thus appears to be expressive of the single thought : True blessedness is not with the outwardly enviable, but the inwardly, however wretched in men's eyes. As usual, in such cases, the nearer we come to the original the greater is the simplicity and self-consistency of the thought. It answers the question, Wherein lies the blessedness of the kingdom ? not, What must be done to attain it?

The general superiority of the Lucan form does not, of course, exclude occasional Matthæan superiority in detail, as where Luke also inserts in v. 21 twice, and in v. 25 twice (β text once) an explanatory νῦν ; in v. 22 the clauses ὅταν μισήσωσιν ὑμᾶς καὶ ἀφορίσωσιν ὑμᾶς and ἕνεκεν ἐμοῦ in v. 23, ἐν ἐκείνῃ τῇ ἡμέρᾳ, and γὰρ and οἱ πατέρες αὐτῶν both here and in v. 26 (a text).

For the discussion of these and similar details see Appendix B.

K

(3) *The Two Preliminary Parables*

Mt. 5 : 13–16 = Mk. 9 : 50ᵃ ; 4 : 21 = Lk. 14 : 34–35;
8 : 16 = 11 : 33

The two parables setting forth (here) the
importance to the world of the disciples' faith-
fulness, are introduced by Matthew at this
point because of the beatitudes (taken as de-
scriptive of the true disciple). The admission
of the woes of course destroys this connection,
which was in reality fictitious, since the meaning assigned by Matthew to both beatitudes and
parables, a meaning on which the connection
depends, is inexact. The context of the discourse itself accordingly excludes them, and as
Mark and Luke both give them elsewhere
(Luke gives the second in two places), it is
certain that they are really stray *logia* attached
by Matthew[ii], or Matthew[iii].

Of the parable of the Salt become Tasteless
(such is its real significance) in the Markan
setting we must say the same. Its only connection with Mk. 9 : 49, 50ᵇ is the bare word
" salt," which is used in quite a different metaphor both before and after. Mk. 9 : 49 would
seem to be a stray *logion* on the seasoning effect

of persecution (cf. 2 Tim. 2 : 1, 3). In 50^b salt
is a metaphor for pungent criticism. Use your
powers of criticism on your own selves (em-
phatic ἑαυτοῖς) ; toward one another keep
peace (cf. Rom. 14 : 13). Luke's setting, as
Wendt has seen,* is correct. The parable is a
warning against weariness in well-doing drawn
from the experience of Palestinian housekeepers,
whose salt, having a large admixture of im-
purities in the shape of white, insoluble " salts,"
when exposed to dampness disappeared, leaving
the tasteless and worthless residuum. The sense
is parallel to Mk. 4 : 17. While Luke's literary
setting is correct, the historical connection is
doubtless approximately Mark's ; for both forms
of the story in this gospel connect with Jesus'
prediction of his fate in Jerusalem a warning to
his disciples of the need to renounce all for the
kingdom. Mk. 8 : 31–33, 34–9 : 1 = Mk. 9 : 30–
32, 43–50.

Wendt also regards the reading καλὸν οὖν τὸ
ἅλας as derived from Mk. 9 : 50, preferring the
Matthæan form ὑμεῖς ἐστὲ τὸ ἅλας τῆς γῆς. It
would be well in that case to follow Wendt's

* *Op. cit.*, p. 125. See below, Appendix C.

own principle of the pairing of parables, and follow Matthew to the further extent of adding at least 5 : 14[a] and 16 ὑμεῖς ἐστε τὸ φῶς τοῦ κόσμου, οὕτως λαμψάτω κτλ.

For the saying on hiding the lamp (or the city on a hill) we have a choice of two other connections, that of Mk. 4 : 21, followed by Luke in 8 : 16, and that of Lk. 11 : 33. The latter is clearly incorrect ; for the illustration of the proper use of truth, to which the saying is clearly adapted, has none but a superficial and mnemonic connection with the warning to follow the inward light as against pretentious human authorities, Lk. 11 : 34–36. Mark's setting, however, is not necessarily correct because Matthew's and Luke's are incorrect. In fact the *logion* in Mark is appended along with 4 : 22 in a connection which is certainly not original. Mk. 4 : 10–25 as a whole constitutes an interruption to the context of 4 : 1–9, 26–34, in which vv. 11–12 are a first interpolation * (the *agraphon* μυστήριον ἐμὸν ἐμοὶ καὶ τοῖς υἱοῖς τοῦ οἴκου μου, Clem. Alex. *Strom.* v. 10 : 69, and *Clem. Hom.* xix. 20, taken together with Is. 6 : 9

* See *s.v.* Gospels, *Encycl. Bibl.*, p. 1866.

as employed in Rom. 11 : 8). The interpolator takes ἠρώτων τὰς παραβολάς (properly to be understood from v. 34) as if = διὰ τί ἐν παραβολαῖς λαλεῖς αὐτοῖς (Mt. 13 : 10). This interpolated " hard saying " on the " hiding of Jesus' teaching " in the parables has then probably led to the attachment of the other *logia* in 21–25 by way of antidote. The most we can say for the original setting of that on hiding the lamp (city) is that it would seem to have been an exhortation to the disciples to court rather than fear publicity, perhaps that in which the associated *logion* Mk. 4 : 22 appears in Mt. 10 : 26 f.

(4) *The Higher Righteousness*

Mt. 5 : 17–20 = Lk. 16 : 17 +

The originality of 5 : 17, 20 needs no further defence. The question regarding this section of the Matthæan discourse concerns the two *logia* of vv. 18–19, the former of which appears also in Lk. 16 : 17. It here purports to explain (γάρ) the πληρῶσαι of v. 17. If correctly, the most that can be said against the connection is to declare vv. 18–19 superfluous ; if incorrectly,

we must seek a better connection for the *logion*,
if not for its companion, v. 19, as well.

Most critics regard these two sayings on the
permanency of the law, and the relative value of
destructive and constructive reformation, as interpolated.   The fact that Luke gives the former
elsewhere is inconclusive, because Luke omits
for his own reasons the whole section, though
showing acquaintance with it.   In fact his very
next *logion* (16 : 18 = Mt. 5 : 32), which he
makes to follow directly upon this, is certainly
part of the omitted material, and the Lucan
connection of both *logia* is most artificial
(Lk. 16 : 16, "The law and the prophets were
until John ").   We must decide, therefore, on
internal evidence.

The language of Mt. 5 : 18 ($\gamma\acute{\epsilon}\nu\eta\tau\alpha\iota$), even if
we allow no weight at all on this point to the
Lucan form ($\pi\epsilon\sigma\epsilon\hat{\iota}\nu$), certainly suggests that the
"fulfilment" meant by the evangelist who ap-
pends the saying to $\pi\lambda\eta\rho\hat{\omega}\sigma\alpha\iota$ is not that of
renovation by broader and deeper interpreta-
tion, but in action, by obedience ; and we are
reminded that in 8 : 2–4 Matthew [iii] makes the
incident he takes from Mk. 1 : 40–45 follow

immediately after the Sermon, in spite of the absurdity then involved in the injunction of secrecy (cf. Mt. 8 : 1, and 4ª), apparently to illustrate how obediently Jesus " fulfilled " the law.* But the antitheses which follow show that such is not the meaning of the πληρῶσαι of v. 17, but rather " fulfilment " in exposition by enlargement of the content. Moreover, it surely was not Jesus' design to declare that the time would come when every minutest prescription of the *Torah* would be implicitly *obeyed*. It is, however, a frequent assurance of Jesus to his followers that the things concerning himself in Moses and the prophets ("the law" in the broader sense of Scripture) should have their *fulfilment*. If reduced to conjecture for the original connection of this *logion*, we shall do far better, therefore, to take it in this sense of " coming to pass," connecting it with the

---

* Compare the characteristic addition Mt. 3 : 15, " It becometh us to fulfil all righteousness." In other words, the baptism of repentance is indeed meaningless in my case and the relation of baptizer to baptized inappropriate, but as an act of righteousness, an *opus operatum*, we should go through it. An impossible sentiment in the mouth of Jesus; cf. Mk. 2 : 19.

eschatological discourse, or perhaps regarding it as simply a different version of Mk. 13 : 31. The essential nature of the figure is identical with Jer. 31 : 35–37, and it would seem probable that Jesus employed it similarly. We might even conjecture that in the original utterance the form was not " my word," but, as in the O. T. passages generally, " the word of the Lord." In either case the thing absolutely assured is the fulfilment of the " sure mercies of David," and the establishment of the " new covenant."

In 5 : 19 it is not apparent that we have anything out of harmony with the remaining context. That the principle is authentic is demonstrable from the certainly historical *agraphon* on the man working on the Sabbath (Lk. 6 : 5 β text), and from Rom. 14 : 13–23, not to speak of the many instances in which Jesus showed how one might " do and teach the law " even while practising the larger righteousness (*e.g.* Lk. 11 : 41). It is true that the verse would not be missed if removed from between 17 and 20 ; but if a genuine λόγιον its position here is at least admissible on the in-

terpretation of Beyschlag.* The contrast of
καταλῦσαι and πληρῶσαι in v. 17 would receive
thus an explanation in real harmony with the
antitheses which follow. To "relax" (λῦσαι,
cf. καταλῦσαι, v. 17) would be to show by example and teaching that a commandment is
obsolete; to "fulfil" would be to show by
example and teaching how to truly venerate the
past. Both are needful services, but one is
"least," the other "great."

Holtzmann's † objections, fatal as they are
to v. 18, scarcely affect v. 19, and a separation seems really to be required by the difference in sense of γένηται ("come to pass") and
ποιήσῃ ("perform"). The most serious would
be the argument that v. 19 militates against
that very distinction of greater and lesser elements of the Law emphasized elsewhere in
the discourse, *e.g.* vv. 23–24. But is it

* " Among these least commandments there is no mere
empty, vain husk without a kernel to be thrown away.
In each there is a divine thought, an imperishable idea,
which must come to its rights before the letter be allowed
to perish." *New Test. Theol.*, I, p. 110.

† *New Test. Theol.*, I, p. 152.

really the fact that the expression "one of these least commandments" is *opposed* to the distinction?

On the clause ἤ τοὺς προφήτας, v. 17, see Appendix B (2).

(5) *First Antithesis, Murder* vs. *the Spirit of Hatred*

Mt. 5 : 21–26 = Lk. 12 : 57–59

The impropriety of the connection of the warning to impenitent Israel to be reconciled ere too late with its divine adversary, whose impending judgment is to be read in the signs of the times, Mt. 5 : 25–26 = Lk. 12 : 57–59, with that on the superiority of reconciliation (with a brother) to sacrifice, and with the antitheses of the new righteousness generally, is so manifest to every reader of the Lucan context, that we need only refer to Appendix C, vii, p. 247, so far as these verses are concerned. But is the preceding *logion*, 5 : 23–24, on reconciliation with a brother, rightly placed?

We have indeed no parallel report on authority of which we might assign it a different connection, but the connection with the illustrative antithesis is certainly of the loosest, whereas the symmetry of structure of the whole discourse forbids the supposition of such digressions. Jesus was giving illustrations of the higher righteousness of the kingdom, as against scribal casuistic ethics. Did he digress to illustrate the remotely connected principle of the greater importance of humanity than ceremonial? It is far more probable that the connection is owing to the evangelist, whose frequent additions we have already had occasion to note. From what context it may ultimately have been derived is a more difficult question. We should naturally think of Mt. 22 : 40 (cf. Mk. 12 : 33) ; or perhaps better of Mt. 18 : 5–6, 10–14, as the preceding context. If our *logion* were there inserted, 18 : 15 ff. would follow appropriately.*

On the emended form of 5 : 22, conforming to that of the second antithesis (vv. 27–28, 31–32), see Appendix B, and *Journ. of Bib. Lit.*, 1892, i, p. 131, " Note on Mt. 5 : 21–22," by John P. Peters.

---

* The rule of discipline, Mt. 18: 16–17, cannot, in present form, be genuine; but the underlying principle, Win thy brother (v. 15), may.

(6) *Second Antithesis, Adultery* vs. *Impure Thought*

Mt. 5 : 27–32 = Mt. 18 : 6, 8–9 = Mk. 9 : 42–49 = Lk. 17 : 2 + Mt. 19 : 9 = Mk. 10 : 10–11 = Lk. 16 : 18

Wendt,* although recognizing the necessity of removing from the Matthæan context of v. 39 the *logion* on the *hand* that causes stumbling, as having no real relation to the antithesis of purity of thought, *vs.* purity of action only, thinks it needful to retain the *logion* (v. 29) on the *eye* that causes stumbling, on the ground that " Jesus adduces examples in most of the other portions of this section, of how his commands surpass the earlier." But we have already had occasion to remove vv. 23–24 to which reference appears to be made, so that this argument is inverted. Moreover, the attempt to divide the saying on sacrificing that which is most precious if it become an obstacle to salvation into two utterances on separate occasions is like attributing to different poems the two halves of any familiar stanza.

One must then not only consider the strophe and antistrophe of Mt. 5 : 29 and 30 to be the

* *Op. cit.,* p. 59.

work of the evangelist, or of some predecessor in the field; but must also consider that the association of the two in Mk. 9 : 43–48 is the result of a second independent attempt to combine in poetic form these same two independent *logia*. And over and above this we have the testimony of Matthew himself in 18 : 6–9, where he copies Mk. 9 : 42–47, to this more original form, wherein *three* members, hand, *foot*, and eye, were used as examples.

Accordingly, we have here to do with an independent *logion*, somewhat abridged in Mt. 18 : 8–9 from the highly rhetorical form of Mark, with threefold strophe and thrice recurrent refrain βληθῆναι εἰς γέενναν, and still further abridged in Mt. 5 : 29–30. The examples of similar twofold or threefold strophic utterance elsewhere in Jesus' teaching (Mt. 6 : 1–18; 11 : 7–10, 20–24) strongly support the originality of the Markan form. But if so we shall be compelled to distinguish between Matthew[iii], who has incorporated Mk. 9 : 42–47 in Mt. 18 : 6–9, and Matthew[ii], who inserts it in 5 : 29–30.*

* See my *Introd. to N. T. Lit.*, p. 202, and Soltau, *Eine Lücke der Synoptischen Forschung*, 1900.

For (*a*) while it is not at all inconceivable that the duplication should escape notice if the *logion* had already been incorporated by an earlier hand in a large section, such as the Sermon on the Mount, it is less probable that the *same* editor would deliberately insert it *twice*, not without considerable change of form. Accordingly, the incorporation of 5 : 29–30 into its present context will have preceded the taking up of the discourse as a whole, and of Mk. 9 : 33–50 into our Matthew. Moreover, (*b*) Matthew[ii], in 5 : 29–30, shows decided appreciation of strophic form, and while he destroys the threefold strophe of Mark, is able to produce a twofold strophe of artistic type. But Matthew[iii], as we have seen, makes havoc of this artistic structure by his additions, and can hardly have had appreciation for rhetorical form.

But is it possible to form a reasonable conjecture as to the original connection of the *logion* ?

Certainly not from the preceding context of Mark. Here 9 : 43–48 is appended to the warning against "stumbling" (σκανδαλίζειν) a "little one," simply because of the mnemonic word σκανδαλίζειν. Inner connection there is none whatever. Moreover, the warning against stumbling the "little ones that believe," by which, as we may easily see from the form of the *logion* in *Clem. Rom.* xlvi, 8 (Οὐαὶ τῷ ανθρώπῳ ἐκείνῳ · καλὸν ἦν αὐτῷ εἰ οὐκ ἐγεννήθη ἢ ἕνα τῶν ἐκλεκτῶν μου σκανδαλίσαι κτλ.), are not meant children, but those *weak in the faith*, is attached by the merest mnemonic relation to the saying, Mk. 9 : 37, 41, about "receiving a little *child*." Mk. 9 : 33–50 is thus seen to be, for the most part, a mere agglomeration of stray *logia;* for we have seen above how purely fictitious is the connection of the sayings about salt and fire, 9 : 49–50.

If, then, we dissolve the fictitious connection between the *logion* on Causing the Weak to Stumble, and that on Stopping at no Sacrifice for Salvation, we have for the former the evidence of both Matthew and Luke that it came from the connection of the teaching concerning Duty toward those "who are of the Household of the Faith" (10–14, 15, 21–35), which is given very briefly indeed in Lk. 17 : 1–4, but forms the basis of the entire chapter Mt. 18, though certain intrusive elements here are derived from Mark, as we have seen in the case of vv. 8–9, and certain others, as vv. 16–20, from other sources.*

But where place the *logion* on stopping at no sacrifice for salvation. Here Luke deserts us entirely, having absolutely no trace of the saying, though several closely related warnings (*e.g.* 13: 22–25) ; and Matthew, as we have seen, vacillated between two contexts, neither of which can be right. We have one resort left, the succeeding context in Mark. It is true that v. 49[b] is shown by the earlier texts to be a mere gloss, and even 49[a] has much the same character of an addendum to v. 48 suggested by the recurrence of the word πῦρ. But, however it may be with these four words, πᾶς γὰρ πυρὶ ἁλισθήσεται, 50[a],

---

* For brevity's sake we are compelled to omit from Appendix C this discourse on Duty to Members of the Household of Faith, which Réville has perceived to be one of the seven principal discourses of our first gospel, (i.) the New Law, 5: 3–7: 27; (ii.) Apostolic Instructions, 9: 37–38; 10: 5–16, 33–42; (iii.) Foes, 11: 7–19, 21–30; 12: 24–25, 28, 30, 37–39; (iv.) Parables of the Kingdom, 13: 1–52; (v.) Relationships within the Kingdom, 18: 2–7, 10–23; 20: 1–16; 21: 23–27; 22: 1–6, 8–14; (vi.) Woes, 23; (vii.) Eschatology, 24: 11–12, 26–28, 37–51; 25.

as we have seen, is a warning against faint-heartedness supported by reference to the destruction of worthless material. In Lk. 14 : 34 it follows upon the two parables on counting the cost, which end, "So, therefore, whosoever he be that renounceth not all that he hath, he cannot be my disciple." Luke has employed this context of 14 : 25–35 to forestall a misuse of the parable of the great supper, 14 : 15–24, and we cannot say what originally came before it ; very possibly the answer "Strive to enter in," to the question, "Lord, are there few that be saved?" Lk. 13 : 22–30. But enough that Mark's connection of the warning, Stop at no Sacrifice, with that of the Tasteless Salt is vindicated. We have in Lk. 14 : 25–35 a reasonable context, even if we do not add Lk. 13 : 22–30. Both belong to the period when Jesus' followers, having forsaken all (Mk. 10 : 28), are on their way to the great crisis in Jerusalem.

On the readings of Mt. 5 : 32 (=Mk. 10 : 10–12=Mt. 19 : 9=Lk. 16 ; 18) and of the succeeding antitheses of duty toward man, Mt. 5 : 33–48, 7 : 12 = Lk. 6 : 27–36 +, see Appendix B (4), (5), and (6).

L

(7) *The Three Antitheses of Duty toward God*

Mt. 6: 1–18=Mk. 11: 25, Lk. 11: 1–4

Further argument is needless to show that the true occasion for the Lord's Prayer is that given by Luke, and although no parallel to Mt. 6: 7–8 appears, no one is at a loss to understand the omission by our Gentile evangelist. Accordingly, since the symmetry of the antitheses is no less strongly opposed to their presence in the Matthæan connection, than the integrity of the thought, which forbids digressions into general instruction on how to pray acceptably, we exclude the whole passage, vv. 7–15, assigning 7 (8 duplicates 6: 32 and is redactional), 9–13 (in the simpler fivefold Lucan form)* to the Lucan discourse on Prayer.†

But Lk. 18: 1–8, although placed by our evangelist at the end of an eschatological section 17: 20–37, because, as he rightly perceives, the widow who importunately calls for justice is the widowed 'daughter of Zion' (cf. v. 7) has its own explanatory introduction (v. 1) which clearly and, as would seem, correctly stated its

* See Lecture, p. 79. † See Appendix C, 1, p. 183.

didactic intent; and this connects the parable by closer ties with Lk. 11 : 1–13. Its subject is identical: Persistence in Prayer. The mere fact that its illustration is in line with 17 : 20–37 is not enough to justify divorce from the discourse on Prayer. As to date the most that can be said is that the occasion of the discourse seems to be later than the choice of the Twelve, Mk. 3 : 7–12, perhaps later than the death of the Baptist; but earlier than the crisis in Galilee, Mk. 7 : 1–24, after which general religious teaching was less in the minds of the disciples than the special problems of the immediate situation.

But the saying on forgiveness, 14–15, has only a fortuitous relation to the teachings on prayer. To classify it with these is as if one should place the saying on Reconciliation being better than Sacrifice, Mt. 5 : 24, in the category of teachings regarding true sacrifice. In fact the two just named are companion utterances, as will be seen as soon as we bring Mt. 6 : 14–15 into its true connection among the teachings on Duty to those who are of the Household of the Faith, Reconciliation and Forgiveness, in Mt. 18.

For the connection in Mark is a typical example of mere mnemonic association, so common in the occasional *logia* of our second
gospel, as if sayings attached on the margin had
become incorporated.* In fact the Markan
connection (καὶ ὅταν στήκετε προσευχόμενοι)
strongly suggests derivation from Matthew [ii] or
Matthew [iii]. In Mt. 18, the *logion* 6 : 14–15
will have formed the conclusion of the parable
on forgiveness, 18 : 21–35.

(8) *Earthly against Heavenly Wealth*

Mt. 6 : 19–34 = Lk. 12 : 13–34; 11 : 34–35; 16 : 1–9, 11–
13, 19–25

Additional argument to prove the correctness
of Luke's setting, as against Matthew's, for this

---

* The whole of Mk. 11 : 20–25 is made up of such
debris. The *logion* 22–24 comes from the connection
Mt. 17 : 19–20 where its sense is as true to the principles of Jesus as in that of Mk. 11 : 20–21 it would be
false. So of 25 where forgiveness is *not* inculcated as a
means of getting our prayers answered. Verses 20–21
form simply an editorial link to connect with 11 : 12–14,
which the evangelist fails to understand as symbolic
action of the prophetic type, and thus assumes to require an actual and visible effect. The incident of the
fig tree is complete in 11 : 12–14[a]; cf. Mt. 21 : 18–22
(N.B. παραχρῆμα).

great discourse as a whole will be needless for those who admit the principles of criticism and wasted on those who do not. For the discourse as a whole, in its larger Lucan connection, we refer the reader to Appendix C, II, p. 186.

But the two *logia* on Single-mindedness (?) and Serving two Masters, Mt. 6 : 22-24, do not occur in the discourse on Earthly *vs*. Heavenly Wealth, Lk. 12 : 13-34, but elsewhere in Luke, the former in connection with Jesus' defence against the blasphemy of the scribes from Jerusalem, Lk. 11 : 14-36, the latter in connection with an independent discourse on wealth and what it can and cannot do, in Lk. 16. Apart from the inappropriateness of the whole teaching in a discourse on the New Righteousness, we have two reasons for thinking the setting of Luke correct, at least for Mt. 6 : 22-23. (*a*) It is difficult to discover in it any relation to the context (earthly *vs*. heavenly riches) unless taken as contrasting with v. 24, in the sense : Make the heavenly wealth the undivided object of your pursuit. Do not divide your service between it and Mammon. In Matthew's conception the "single eye," therefore, is that of the servant of Ps. 123 : 2, unswervingly fixed on the master from whom the reward is to come. But while such a conception may very well have led to the insertion of both *logia* here, it certainly fails to do justice to the saying on the "lamp of the body," if indeed the general teaching, Make the heavenly reward your undivided object, be not on general principles too meretricious to accord with the unselfish teachings of Jesus (cf. Mk. 8 : 35, and parallels). In this interpretation everything turns on the word ἁπλοῦς, as against the δυσὶ κυρίοις of v. 24, "single" *vs.* "double" service. But if Matthew's were the original meaning, the contrasting adjective in the negative half of the *logion*, v. 23, describing the eye as it must not be, should not be πονηρός. *Double* sight may not be a correct antithesis on account of the "doubleness" of normal sight, but we should at least expect some such epithet as "wandering" or "inconstant." The use of πονηρός by both authorities indicates that the "simplicity" meant is not *singleness* vs. *duality*, but singleness in the sense of honesty ; *integrity* vs. *duplicity*. Moreover, the condition of inward light or darkness is not what we should expect where the object sought is not clearness of vision, but heavenly reward. It is in the Lucan connection, Blind Leaders *vs*. the Inward Guidance, that it becomes appropriate to say: Inward light is given to those who preserve *integrity* of mind. The true sense of the saying, accordingly, is that which it has in the context of Lk. 11: 29–32, 34–36.

We have indeed a difficult problem in the disentanglement from the two accounts of Matthew (Mt. 9 : 32–34 ; 12 : 22–45, and 16 : 1–12), two of Mark (Mk. 3 : 22–30 ; 8 : 11–21, and 7 : 1–23), one of Luke (Lk. 11 : 14–54 ; 12 : 1, 10), and two of John (Jn. 6 : 30 ff. connected with 9 : 40 ff.) of the great philippic of Jesus in Capernaum against the scribes and Pharisees. But of one thing we may be fairly certain, the saying on the lamp of the body *vs*. the inward light, was uttered, as we learn from Lk. 11 : 29–32, 34–36, in rebuke of the " evil and adulterous " demand for a sign from heaven, and the " simplicity " of eye on which inward illumination is conditioned, is not that of the servant intent on his reward, but of him who

seeks the right path for himself or others. It is
the simplicity of the childlike and teachable
spirit, because of which Jesus could thank the
Father that though hidden from the wise and
prudent, his gospel was revealed unto babes. It
is *integrity* of mind, as opposed to the *duplicity*
of the "hypocritical" scribes and Pharisees,
who, because they deemed their own religious
leadership to be threatened by the new prophet,
had covertly (Mt. 12:25) given currency to
their blasphemous verdict, "He casteth out
devils by Beelzebub," then queried why Jesus
and the Twelve kept not "the tradition of the
elders," and finally opposed Jesus' preaching of
warning against impending judgment with the
demand of "a sign from heaven."

For (*b*) that the "evil eye" which is darkened,
is that of the "blind Pharisee," and blinder
scribe who assumes to "lead the blind," not that
of him who merely is divided in his service, is
also suggested by Mark's narrative of this momentous encounter (Mk. 7:1–23), where, after
explaining wherein real defilement consists, we
have enumerated among the faults of those who
outwardly are clean, but inwardly full of all

uncleanness, the " evil eye " and " blasphemy " that had just been shown by " the scribes who came down from Jerusalem."

If thus we are driven to separate Mt. 6 : 22–23 from v. 24, placing the former with Luke in the Denunciation at Capernaum, we may perhaps effect compensation as regards v. 24. The saying on Simplicity of Heart, taken in the sense of Singleness of Service, has clearly been drawn in to the discourse on the Rewards of Heaven by that on Divided Service, Mt. 6 : 24 = Lk. 16 : 13. How then came the *logion* on serving God and Mammon to be inserted here? Manifestly not because of the mere δυσὶ κυρίοις, since it was not here. But bring the saying into relation with its larger connection of Lk. 16 : 1–13, 14–15, 19–25, and it becomes intelligible. It is true the connection of the *logia* in Lk. 16 : 10–13 appears somewhat broken, v. 10 introducing possibly a foreign element.*

Yet there is at least no incompatibility between v. 13 and 1–9, 11–12 ; for the warning of the parable, "Use fleeting wealth as a means to

---

* Perhaps the original refrain answering to Lk. 19 : 17 = Mt. 25 : 23, which will have stood in place of 19 : 27.

higher ends while it is in your hands," is not remote from the teaching, " Beware lest you allow it to become an end in itself in rivalry with God."

But here appears an affinity between the *logion* on divided service and the discourse on heavenly wealth which quite disappears in the Matthæan form. The wealth ($\mu\alpha\mu\mu\acute{\omega}\nu$) of unrighteousness, belonging as it does to the Prince of this world (Lk. 4 : 6), " faileth " ($\dot{\epsilon}\kappa\lambda\acute{\iota}\pi\epsilon\iota$, Lk. 16 : 9). The specified characteristic of the heavenly treasure is that it *does not fail* (Mt. 6 : 19–20).

How then comes Matthew[iii] to insert into the discourse on the " Treasure in heaven that faileth not," a verse which in the larger connection of Lk. 16 : 1–13 we find attached to a parable on the use of " the mammon that belongs to unrighteousness," which though it " fails " can be made a means to " eternal habitations " ($\alpha\dot{\iota}\omega\nu\acute{\iota}o\nu\varsigma$ $\sigma\kappa\eta\nu\acute{\alpha}\varsigma$) ; and yet himself quite overlook this relation and substitute a fictitious one? Must it not be that v. 24 (save for what belongs to it in Lk. 16 : 1–9 (10–12?)) is, after all, substantially in right relation to Mt. 6 : 19–21? Will it not have been because Matthew[iii] found the verse (*plus* somewhat more too diverse from his theme of the heavenly reward to be utilized) in this connection, that he placed it here, inserting before it 6 : 22–23 to form the contrast Single *vs.* Divided Service?   But if so, then in Luke also there has been to some extent a separation of connected material by the insertion of other less directly related.   For the great discourse on the abiding heavenly wealth in Lk. 12 : 13–34, part of which is adopted in Mt. 6 : 19–34, is separated from that on How to use the fleeting Wealth of the World, Lk. 16 : 1–13, by miscellaneous material extending from 12 : 35 to the end of chapter 15.   The parable of the rich man and Lazarus, to which some hand has appended a totally foreign addition * in vv. 26–31, is a warning against judgment by outward appearance, and therefore cannot tolerate the intervention of the three stray *logia*, vv. 16–18, two of which we have already located elsewhere, between it and v. 15, which it serves to illustrate. The originality of the editorial connection, v. 14,

---

* See my article, "The Transfiguration Story," in *Am. Journ. of Theol.*, April, 1902; and Jülicher, *Gleichnissreden, ad loc.*

has indeed been doubted on the ground that
avarice was not a characteristic sin of the Pharisees. But the genuineness of φιλάργυροι ὑπάρχοντες may be questioned without rejecting the
whole verse. Therefore, until more decisive evidence appears against our evangelist's historical
settings than we have yet found, we must regard
14-15, 19-25 as a unit, the conclusion of the
great discourse on Earthly *vs.* Heavenly Wealth,
Lk. 12 : 13-34, 16 : 1-9, 11-13.

(9) *How the New Standard of Righteousness should be applied*

(1) To self, not others, Mt. 7 : 1-27 + = Lk. 6 : 37-49 +

The Application of the great discourse on the
Higher Righteousness falls naturally into three
divisions. (1) It is a standard for self-correction, not for censoriousness ; * (2) the refor-

---

* In this connection it is worth while to note the
concluding instructions of Paul to the πνευμάτικοι (leaders of the church) in Galatia. They are to restore the
erring in a spirit of meekness looking to themselves lest
they also be tempted. It is somewhat significant that
this echo of the concluding section of the Discourse on
the New Law should be inculcated by Paul as a "ful-
filling of *the law of Christ,*" Gal. 6 : 1-4.

mation must be from the root, not superficial;
(3) deeds not words will tell.

Of these Luke preserves only (2) and (3) in-
tact. He employs (1) as he employs elements
from the antithesis on Retaliation (Lk. 6 : 29, 30,
34, 35 = Mt. 5 : 40–42) to fill out the reduced
dimensions of that statement of the Higher
Righteousness in exclusively affirmative form,
6 : 27–38, which he substitutes for the antitheses as a whole. Such at least would seem to be
the more probable explanation of the connection of 37–38ª with the preceding verses. For
while they appear to offer a motive for the disinterested goodness inculcated, namely, " kindness will breed kindness," the very suggestion of
such a motive is more or less incongruous with
the commendation of purely disinterested goodness. At least the level of the sublime saying,
vv. 35–36, wherein true goodness is commended
as the imitation of Him who gives without the
possibility of return, is hardly maintained if we
add, " For men will do as much again for you,"
Lk. 6 : 37, 38ª, must therefore be derived from
another context, possibly that of Mt. 18, for the
duty inculcated in v. 37 is forgiveness.

Again the two *logia*, Lk. 6 : 39–40, have certainly a fictitious connection.   As the paragraph
stands the sense must be, " Beware of assuming
to guide when not yourself enlightened ; the
result will be that the pupil becomes as his
teacher."   To this then is subjoined the saying
on removing a splinter from a brother's eye.
But it can hardly be admitted that Jesus should
have applied to any disciple of his own, however
overhasty to assume the functions of a teacher,
the epithet of " blind guide " which he applied
in withering denunciation to the scribes.   Moreover, we cannot be mistaken as to the sense of
Mt. 7 : 3–5 = Lk. 6 : 41–42.   Both witnesses
agree in placing it here, and the *logion* itself
clearly shows that it is not so much a warning
against assuming to *teach* without adequate
preparation, as a warning against assuming to
judge.   We must, therefore, follow Matthew in
excluding these *logia*, Lk. 6 : 37^{bc}, 38^a, 39, 40.
We have, indeed, no parallel elsewhere to 37^{bc},
38^a, though kindred teachings are not wanting
(cf. Mt. 18 : 23–35 ; Lk. 7 : 36–50 ; Jn. 7 : 55–
8 : 11 — originally " Lucan "), so that at best we
can give it but a very loose connection.   But

6 : 39 is a parallel to Mt. 15 : 14, and 6 : 40 to
Mt. 10 : 24–25. In both cases the Matthæan
setting is preferable and is supported by the
testimony of John (6 : 39 = Jn. 9 : 40–41 ; 6 : 40
= Jn. 13 : 16 ; 15 : 20). The two verses are
not quite in harmony with the context, which is
not a warning against ambition to be teachers,
but against the fault-finding spirit. Thus in Luke
the sayings have the appearance of *logia* attached
from floating tradition.* In Mt. 15 : 14 and
10 : 24–25 they give their true sense.

Per contra, Matthew's insertion of 7 : 6 can
be accounted for only by the evangelist's desire
to warn against misdirected zeal in applying
gospel truth, but is too remote from the real
subject to be authentic in the connection. If
genuine, as we have no need to doubt, it formed,
perhaps, a fragment, orally preserved, of the
directions to the Twelve when sent to preach the
kingdom, Mt. 10 : 14–15. The rhetorical form
is, of course, a *chiasmus*, " lest they (the swine)
tread them (the pearls) under foot, and they
(the dogs) turn and rend you." It is safer to

---

* Cf. Wendt, *op. cit.*, p. 65, and Weiss, *Matthäusev.*,
p. 206.

follow the actual precedent of Mt. 15 : 26 (=
Mk. 7 : 27 ; cf. 15 : 5) than to reason on *a priori*
grounds that " Jesus cannot have been unwilling
his gospel should be preached to any class," and
connect the saying (so O. Holtzmann) with Mt.
16 : 20. The connection of the *second* sending
of the Twelve, Mt. 10 : 16–42, however, seems
more probable than that of Mt. 10 : 1–15. The
dogs and swine will then be, not heathen generally, but persecutors.

Why the greater part of the discourse on
Prayer, Lk. 11 : 1–13, not already taken up in
Mt. 6 : 9–13, should be inserted next by
Matthew [iii] in 7 : 7–11, is hard to say. Connection of thought is undiscoverable. Perhaps the
need of finding room somewhere for such indispensable teaching, and the general character the
discourse assumes in our evangelist's mind, was
reason enough for throwing it in here. Defence
of the Lucan connection is superfluous.*

So also with 7 : 12 which Luke gives correctly
both as to place and form. Verse 12[b] is an addition (cf. Lk. 6 : 31) from Mt. 22 : 40, no doubt
from the hand which, by means of a similar addi-

* See Appendix C, I.

tion in 5 : 17, changes the sense to a more general adaptation of the discourse. The summary is in place, as Wendt has seen, after the fourth ethical antithesis, just before the comprehensive fifth.

(10) *Radical Reformation*

Mt. 7 : 13–20 = Lk. 6 : 43–45; 13 : 24–27 +

A more difficult problem confronts us in paragraph (2). According to Wendt the *leitmotif* of the sections (1) Mt. 6 : 1–6, 16–18, (2) 7 : 1–5, (3) 15–19, is "the hypocritical zeal for righteousness" of which one form is (1) outward show in acts of piety; another (2) censoriousness toward others with blindness to one's own faults; a third (3) our present paragraph, ambition to be teachers. Accordingly, his explanation of the employment of the *logion*, 7 : 13–14 = Lk. 13 : 24, as an introduction to the paragraph 15–20, is as follows : Matthew [iii], intending to avail himself of part of the *logion* in 7 : 22–23 = Lk. 13 : 26–27, and wishing to preserve the rest, employed it in this place for lack of a better. It is, indeed, well-nigh as hard to see a real connection of thought between the *logion* and its context here, as easy to see it in its Lucan con-

M

text (Lk. 13 : 22–30). Now the figure of the two gates and two ways is a common one in antiquity, both Jewish and classic.* In answer to the question (Lk. 13 : 23), " Lord, are there few that be saved? " it comes in appropriately in connection with the sayings (here rigidly condensed ; cf. Mt. 24 : 37–25 : 46 and 8 : 11) on exclusion of those who, in their own estimation, are entitled to a place in the kingdom. The Lucan setting is, therefore, correct. But it is hard to see why even such a compiler as Matthew should give it room in a warning against " ambition to teach." If, however, the paragraph is really on Radical Reformation, the saying has a sufficient degree of appropriateness here to account for its insertion.

Now in the Lucan version of the discourse (Lk. 6 : 43–45) there can be no question that radical reformation is in fact the sense. Prophets or teachers are not mentioned. The two kinds of trees are compared respectively to the good and bad man, each of whom manifests in deed (and word?) his real nature. Only the appended

* *Test. of Abraham*, and Johannes ben Zakkai (*Ber.* 28ᵇ); also in the *Tablet* of Kebes.

clause 45^b, ἐκ γὰρ περισσεύματος καρδίας λαλεῖ τὸ στόμα αὐτοῦ suggests anything like the Matthæan sense, and this does not appear in Matthew's version. In fact, it has much the appearance of a scribal addition from Mt. 12 : 34. But Mt. 12 : 33–35 forms a doublet to 7 : 16–18, this time taking the form of Lk. 6 : 43–45, so that here Matthew witnesses against himself. What then is the solution of the puzzle? The intrinsic sense of the *logia* themselves (for there are two, one on judging pretended *teachers* by their fruits, 7 : 15–17, 20, the other on reforming *men* in their nature to secure right action, Lk. 6 : 43, 45) will give us the key. The saying on the good tree *vs.* the rotten has really quite a different bearing from that on plucking grapes from thorns and figs from thistles. The first teaches the indispensableness of a sound *nature*, the second applies a common-sense rule to the discrimination of the worthy from the unworthy *leader*. Now it is only the former which has proper relation to the Sermon on the Mount, so that both 45^b and v. 44 (= Mt. 7 : 16) are alien to this context. But how have they found their way hither, since in Luke the context has no reference to the detection of false leaders? Only the confusion of Mt. 7 : 15–20 with Mt. 12 : 33–35 can explain it. Mt. 7 : 15, 16, 20 and 12 : 34 belong elsewhere.* Jesus undoubtedly warned his disciples against the wolves in sheep's clothing, and gave them this principle of discrimination, " Men gather not grapes from thorns nor figs from thistles ; " but not at this time. The place of this saying is more probably among the warnings for the future of the church, given when Jesus was preparing the Twelve for his impending fate. We are reminded of Mt. 24 : 11–12 ; but the teachers here spoken of are not the special " false prophets " of eschatology, but the " grievous wolves " of Acts 20 : 29.† A better connection is the section on teachers in the church, Mt. 23 : 1–12. It is the mention of tree and fruit which belongs between the paragraph on Self-judging and on Deeds not Words. Matthew may have considered that the judgment which in self-defence we are compelled to exercise upon those who assume to direct us, formed

* See Appendix C, p. 256.

† See, however, Resch, *Agrapha*, Par. 110 and cf. Διδαχή 16: 3.

an appropriate exception to follow after the
warning, " Judge not " ; and combined the two
sayings on fruit-bearing as the test of character. But this combination was antecedent to
Matthew [iii], (*a*) because the connection is with
7 : 1–5 and is interrupted by vv. 6–14 ; and (*b*)
because it has affected Lk. 6 : 43–45, and Luke
shows no acquaintance with Matthew [iii]. Mt.
7 : 17 is, therefore, in the nature of an editorial
link.

Finally, as between the Lucan and Matthæan
setting for Lk. 6 : 43, 45 = Mt. 12 : 33, 35, it is
easy to see that Luke's is correct, for Mt. 7 : 18
cannot stand alone, but requires this teaching to follow it. On the other hand, Jesus as-
suredly did not address the disciples on whom
he had just pronounced the blessings of the
kingdom as a " generation of vipers," γεννήματα
ἐχιδνῶν. Mt. 12 : 34, if not simply compounded
of Mt. 3 : 7 and the proverb ἐκ περισσεύματος
καρδίας λαλεῖ τὸ στόμα, belongs in the Denunciation of Scribes and Pharisees (Mt. 12 : 22–45
and parallels), and is responsible for the displacement of vv. 33 and 35. In compensation
Matthew [iii] appends in 7 : 19–20 a doublet of

3 : 10, and a repetition of v. 16ᵃ. In this paragraph, accordingly, it is substantially the Lucan form which we must follow, omitting 44 and 45ᵇ.

(11) *Deeds not Words*

Mt. 7 : 21–27 = Lk. 6 : 46–49, 13 : 26, 27

Wendt's observation that Mt. 7 : 22–23 has been borrowed from the Lucan context is certainly correct. Warnings against exclusion in the day of judgment are in place in that eschatological section of Luke, to which we have already assigned the counsel to seek timely reconciliation with the great Plaintiff; they have slight relation to a context on proper use of the new standard of righteousness. But over and above this it is inconceivable that Jesus at this period of his ministry, before his Messianic claims had been broached, should have openly referred to himself as judge at the final assize. Accordingly we must recognize that while the substance of Mt. 7 : 21 remains, on the testimony of Lk. 6 : 46, and because the proposition in illustration of which the parable, vv. 24–27 (= Lk. 6 : 47–49), is uttered requires to be stated, its form has been altered to agree with

the eschatological *logion* which follows in v. 22
(ἐροῦσιν . . . κύριε, κύριε; cf. Mt. 25 : 11, 37,
44). Mt. 12 : 50 suggests the form of the last
half of the verse. The Lucan form, 6 : 46,
agrees with the succeeding context (ἀκούων . . .
καὶ ποιῶν), and must accordingly represent the
original.*

(12) *The Colophon and Succeeding Events*

Mt. 7 : 28–29; 8 : 1–13 = Lk. 7 : 1; 5 : 12–16; 7 : 2–10

A comparison of the concluding remark by
which each evangelist Matthew and Luke describes the effect of the great discourse, is of sin-
gular value as evidence of the history of its
transmission during the formative period of
our gospels.

The formula καὶ ἐγένετο ὅτε ἐτέλεσεν ὁ Ἰησοῦς
κτλ. is employed five times in Matthew, each
time as the conclusion of one of the great
masses of discourse material which distinguishes
this gospel (7 : 28; 11 : 1; 13 : 53; 19 : 1;
26 : 1). Sir John Hawkins † has given excellent reasons for regarding it, however, as a
phrase coined not by Matthew [iii], but by an earlier

---

* See Appendix B.   † *Horæ Synopticæ*, p. 132.

compiler.* The first is that " Lk. 7 : 1 ἐπειδὴ
ἐπλήρωσεν πάντα τὰ ῥήματα αὐτοῦ is so closely
parallel in substance, though not in words, to
Mt. 7 : 28 as to suggest a common origin for
them both." We have just seen that there
are phenomena of the text which are unaccountable without a connection between Luke
and Matthew[ii].

We may add to this another conclusion. It
was the work already of this Matthew [ii] to combine the five *Pereqs*, as Sir John felicitously calls
them, with a narrative, and this narrative at least
partly drawn from our Mark. For (1) the formula itself implies that the *Pereqs* were followed
not by new *discourse*, which would make it meaningless, but by *narrative*. (2) In 7 : 28–29 the
formula is combined with Mk. 1 : 22. (3) A
second loan from Mark is made in 8 : 1–4
(= Mk. 1 : 40–44 = Lk. 5 : 12–16), and this, as
we have seen,† absurdly ill placed. Both are
not likely to have been made by the same hand.
We get the same impression (the need to dis-

---

* In point of fact our gospel, as we have seen, is
distinguished not by five but by seven such masses. See
above, Appendix A (6), p. 144.　　　† p. 134.

criminate Matthew[iii] from Matthew[ii]) in 26 : 1,
where the formula is misemployed (ὅτε ἐτέλεσε
τοὺς λόγους . . . εἶπε κτλ.). Moreover, we have
seen that the symmetry of the Sermon on the
Mount is constantly broken without regard for
its beautiful rhetorical balance, and Sir John's
careful investigations bring him to the conclusion
that this earlier compilation was even more highly
characterized than our Matthew (Matthew[iii])
by attention to numerical form and symmetry.

Finally he sees good evidence of an interrelation between Matthew[ii] and Luke. We also,
besides the apparent dependence in Lk. 6 :
43–45, have already noted the remarkable
coincidence of Luke's adoption of the very
same passage in Mark as that chosen by
Matthew for the historical setting of the discourse, and now, since we have found it needful to remove the second loan from Mark
(Mt. 8 : 1–4) as manifestly out of place, discover that in consequence the sequence of
narrative again coincides (Mt. 8 : 5–10, 13
= Lk. 7 : 2–10). Two such coincidences cannot be accidental. Since our Matthew and
Luke are certainly independent, it is either

Matthew[ii] who has borrowed from Luke (or
one of his sources), or *vice versa*. Soltau has
recently come forward with an urgent plea for
the indispensableness of such a Matthew[ii].
Our own independent investigations have shown
the assumption to be entirely correct, so far
as regards the necessity of an intermediate
link to account for the relation of Matthew to
Luke. There was a combination of the *logia*
and Mark before our Matthew; but it merits
quite as much the title of Proto-Luke as
Deutero-Matthew, for some of its material is
of the very bone and flesh of the "special
source" of Luke. Of this type is the present
narrative of the Centurion's Servant, which appears not at all in Mark, but, aside from Mt.
8 : 5–13 = Lk. 7 : 1–10, only in Jn. 4 : 46–54,
and there in widely variant form. In its whole
animus it is distinctively characteristic of what
has been significantly designated "The gospel
of the poor and oppressed," * and in the whole
mode of representation is of a piece with Acts
10 : 1 ff. Moreover, as O. Holtzmann has seen,†

---

* See my *Introduction to the New Testament*, p. 220.

† *Leben Jesu*, 1901, p. 22.

the primary form is the Lucan. That of Matthew
is unmistakably secondary. But Matthew cannot have it from our gospel of Luke, since the
omission of so much else would be unaccountable, not to say the composition of the work
itself. Neither can it be from Mark, as
O. Holtzmann supposes, imagining an accidental omission from our form of the second
gospel; for it has no affinity with, nor place
in Mark. It belonged to that special source of
Luke and Acts whose chief feature is its cham-
pionship of the lowly, the publican and sinner,
the Samaritan, the penitent thief and repentant
harlot, the Gentile and the woman, the widowed
and poor, the lowly and despised. Matthew [iii]
shows appreciation of the bearing of the *logion*,
" I have not seen such faith in Israel," by
attaching the refrain of the eschatological discourse, Lk. 13 : 22–30 = Mt. 24 : 37–25 : 46.
But the very separation of the refrain from its
proper setting (Lk. 13 : 28–30 = Mt. 24 : 51 ;
25 : 30 ; cf. 13 : 42, 50 ; 22 : 13), breaking up
the symmetrical form of Matthew [ii] is evidence
that here we are dealing with a third stage of
the process. The narrative will have run

4 : 18–22 . . . 8 : 14–16 (17), 1ᵇ–13 (cf. Lk.
7 : 1–10 ; Jn. 4 : 46–54 ; 6 : 1 ff.), 18 ff.*

With Mt. 8 : 13 = Lk. 7 : 10 we reach the
end in Matthew of that great section which the
evangelist inserts into the narrative of Mark.
Mt. 8 : 14 resumes the Markan narrative at
the point where it had been dropped after
4 : 18–22,† and proceeds with the chain of ten
mighty works, the pendant to the discourse.
Luke also has reached the end of the section.
Doubtless he derives his ensuing material,
7 : 11–8 : 3, from the same source, but the
connection of his story of the raising of the
widow's son at Nain is not in any degree with

* See my *Introduction to the New Testament*, p. 201.
† The demoniac in the Synagogue at Capernaum, Mk.
1 : 21–28, is purposely omitted. Matthew manifestly
disapproves the theory of Mark that the demons constantly recognized Jesus as the Christ and had to be
silenced (Mk. 1 : 34; 3 : 11–12; cf. Mt. 12 : 16); rightly
judging it, apparently, an unwarranted inference from
the single authentic instance of Mk. 5 : 6–8 (= Mt.
8 : 29). Mk. 1 : 21–28 thus appears to him (rightly so
far as the demoniac's outcry is concerned) a doublet of
5 : 1–20, and is accordingly omitted ; but with the compensation of a *second* demoniac introduced in 8 : 28–34 ;
cf. 9 : 27–31; 20 : 29–34.

the foregoing, but solely with the subsequent account of Jesus' answer to the messengers of the Baptist, bidding them tell John how, among the other works of the Christ, " the dead are raised up."

Here, accordingly, we lay down our immediate task. Not all the conclusions reached are of equal probability. Where Matthew gives one connection for a saying and Luke another we may have reasonable confidence in choosing that which seems best adapted to the intrinsic sense. Much less can be felt when we depart from both, though such cases are rare. Finally, the inferences drawn as to the stages through which the two-fold report of the discourse has come to us, will seem, no doubt, especially precarious. It is but fair to add that our conclusions as to a Matthew [ii] employing a Lucan form of the *logia* rests also on additional evidence more than we have space for here. The student should consult Feine, *Eine vorkanonische Ueberlieferung des Lukas,* 1891, and Soltau, *Eine Lücke der Synoptischen Forschung,* 1899, besides the standard works of Weiss,[*]

* *Markusevangelium* and *Matthæusevangelium.*

Weizsäcker,* and Holtzmann,† and the recent admirable discussions of Hawkins ‡ and
Wernle.§ Further study will doubtless lead to
results divergent in detail from those we here
present; but in the main, and especially in the
more vital question of the earliest attainable
form and connection of the great discourses of
Jesus, we may hope to see them ultimately
confirmed.

* *Evangelische Geschichte.*
† *Synoptische Evangelien.*
‡ *Horæ Synopticæ*, 1899.
§ *Synoptische Frage*, 1899.

APPENDIX B

TEXT-CRITICAL NOTES TO THE DIS-COURSE ON THE HIGHER RIGHT-EOUSNESS

(1) The β text of Mt. 5 : 4–5 inverts the order of these two verses. Verse 5 being simply a reproduction of Ps. 37 : 11, we should probably regard it as a gloss which has crept in at different points from the margin. (See above, Appendix A, p. 127.)

(2) In 6 : 21 Luke has twice, and in v. 25 once, an explanatory νῦν which the parallel in Matthew shows to be editorial. In the same category is the ἐν ἐκείνῃ τῇ ἡμέρᾳ, v. 23. The real contrast is not between present and future, but seeming and real. The words καὶ ὅταν ἀφορίσωσιν ὑμᾶς καὶ ὀνειδίσωσιν and ἕνεκα τοῦ υἱοῦ τοῦ ἀνθρώπου (Mt. ἕνεκεν ἐμοῦ) in v. 22 are also probably added to conform with the treatment actually experienced by the church. The β text of Luke omits καὶ ὀνειδίσωσιν (introduced by the

a text from Matthew), and καὶ ὅταν ἀφορίσωσιν ὑμᾶς clearly imports later conditions. Ἕνεκεν ἐμοῦ (τοῦ υἱοῦ τοῦ ἀνθρώπου) like ψευδόμενοι (Mt. 5 : 11) is a qualification of the statement intended to guard against misuse.

Comparison of the antistrophe, v. 26, confirms this reduction of the overloaded v. 22, and shows the contrast to have been simply between being well and ill spoken of by the world.

In vv. 23 and 26 οἱ πατέρες αὐτῶν is unnecessary and does not appear in v. 26 (β text) nor in the Matthæan form. It looks like an effort to make the statement exact. The β text is also followed in the omission of καὶ κλαύσετε in v. 25, and γάρ in v. 26, on the principle *brevior lectio preferenda*. It is also followed in the omission of πάντες in v. 26, and the reading τοῖς ἐμπεπλησμένοις in v. 25 for ὑμῖν οἱ.

(3) In Mt. 5 : 17 καὶ τοὺς προφήτας appears to be redactional. The contrast οὐ καταλῦσαι ἀλλὰ πληρῶσαι shows that πληρῶσαι is not here used in the sense employed of prophecy. In vv. 19 and 20 we read βασιλεία τοῦ θεοῦ on the principle explained in Appendix A (p. 128). In v. 19 γάρ for οὖν. (See Appendix A, p. 133.)

(4) In Mt. 5 : 22-23 both sense and structure require the emendation of Dr. Peters * above adopted. The strophic form is reproduced in the succeeding antithesis (v. 31) , the contrast is between the heavier offence (εἴπῃ 'Ρακά), on which the Sanhedrin impose a light penalty, and the trivial one (εἴπῃ Μωρέ) on which the heaviest is imposed. Jesus does not, of course, threaten his disciples with the penalties of the Sanhedrin. In 5 : 23 we insert ἐρρέθη to correspond with v. 31. The emendation is not strictly necessary, for Mt. 23 : 18 affords an exact parallel where the corresponding λέγουσι must be tacitly supplied.

(5) The words παρεκτὸς λόγου πορνείας, Mt. 5 : 32, are certainly a gloss. Jesus' attitude on the subject of divorce is clearly set forth in Mk. 10 : 1-12, where this exception is significantly wanting even in the rule (10 : 11-12) ; but again introduced by Matthew[iii]. † Fortunately we have here the authority of Luke as well in the parallel, Lk. 16 : 18, for rejecting the interpolated exception. But the general principle still

* *Journ. of Bib. Lit.,* 1892, i, p. 131.

† See H. J. Holtzmann, *Neutestl. Theol.,* I, p. 142.

N

more emphatically excludes it. The position taken by Jesus is the same as in the case of the request to arbitrate (Lk. 12 : 13). He refuses to occupy the seat of the law-giver or magistrate in the imperfect conditions of the world. No fault is found with Moses for the enactment necessitated by the hardness of men's hearts (wrong social and moral conditions). Only this legislation, whose aim is simply to make the best of things as they are in the interest of the family and home, is not to be confounded with the ideal standard of the kingdom of God, of which Jesus finds the pattern in the utterance of the Creator to the unfallen pair in Paradise. With the ideal conditions alone does Jesus concern himself in formulating the principles of the higher righteousness of the kingdom. The exception παρεκτὸς λόγου πορνείας transforms the principle into a rule, and involves Jesus in the rabbinic debate between the schools of Shammai and Hillel. It is as much out of place in Mt. 5 : 32 as it would be in Gen. 2 : 24.

The reading of Lk. 16 : 18, μοιχεύει for ποιεῖ αὐτὴν μοιχευθῆναι, adopted by Wendt, is commended by its greater simplicity. (See Wendt,

op. cit., p. 59.) In v. 28 αὐτὴν is omitted after
ἐπιθυμῆσαι on the authority of the β text.

(6) The reading of the β text is adopted in
Mt. 5 : 37 instead of ἔστω δὲ ὁ λόγος ὑμῶν ναὶ ναί,
οὔ οὔ. This is indeed the harsher, but may be
accounted for as affected by II Cor. 1 : 17–18.
The sense can hardly be other than as given in
the β text, let your simple affirmation or nega-
tion be conclusive. This form of the text also
omits ὀμόσῃς from v. 36. (See Blass *Evangelium
secundum Matthæum*, 1901, *ad loc.*)

(7) In Mt. 5 : 39 the Lucan form is preferred
in the latter half of the verse on account of
greater conciseness and agreement in form with
verses 40, 42. The sense is identical. Mt.
7 : 12 is placed here on the same authority. The
clause οὗτος γάρ ἐστιν ὁ νόμος καὶ οἱ προφῆται,
wanting in Luke, is substantially a doublet of
22 : 40. It represents too characteristically the
view of Matthew[iii], and is too easily accounted
for redactionally (cf. 5 : 17) to be admitted as
genuine. In Mt. 5 : 42 ἀπὸ σοῦ is omitted before
δανίσασθαι with the β text.

(8) We add between Mt. 5 : 47 and 48 the
verse Lk. 6 : 35, but with much hesitation. It

lengthens the discourse without materially adding to the sense. But the rhetorical structure and balance seem to require it.

(9) In Mt. 6 : 18 the words τῷ ἐν τῷ κρυφαίῳ and ὁ βλέπων ἐν τῷ κρυφαίῳ might seem essential to symmetry with verses 4 and 6. But they are bracketed by Blass,* and it is easier to account for them by supplementation from 4 and 6 than to account for their omission, especially as we have here not κρυπτῷ as in 4, 6, but κρυφαίῳ. In v. 6 σοῦ after ταμεῖον and θύραν and τῷ before the first κρυπτῷ, which are also wanting in some texts, are omitted as unessential.

(10) The briefer form of Lk. 6 : 46–48 commends itself in preference to Mt. 7 : 21–25 except in one respect. The more elaborate description of the building process ἔσκαψεν καὶ ἐβάθυνεν καὶ ἔθηκεν θεμέλιον seems less original than the simple contrast ἐπὶ τὴν πέτραν . . . ἐπὶ τὴν ἄμμον. The Matthæan form is accordingly adopted in 7 : 24^b, 25^b–27.

* *Op. cit.* with a reference to *Beitr. z. Förd. Christl. Theol.*, IV, 17 sq., a work not accessible to me.

APPENDIX C

THE GREATER DISCOURSES OF JESUS
CONNECTED WITH THE SERMON
ON THE MOUNT, IN CONJECTU-
RALLY RESTORED CONTEXT, FORM,
AND ORDER *

I. The Discourse on Prayer

Lk. 11 : 1–13; 18 : 1–8 = Mt. 6 : 7–13; 7 : 7–11

The Occasion

Lk. 11 : 1

Lk. 11 ¹And it came to pass that he was in
a certain place praying; and when he ceased
one of his disciples said to him, Lord, teach

* The principal transpositions of text in this Appendix
are justified in Appendix A, without specific reference
in each case. For omissions and other changes of reading, and for critical results otherwise embodied in the
text of the greater discourses outside the Sermon on the
Mount, resort has been had to a few simple typographical devices. Narrative material, such as the evangelist's
description of the occasion of the discourse, is double

us to pray, even as John also taught his disciples. ² And he said unto them, —

leaded. The discourse of Jesus is set in. Where it
seems to exhibit the lyric structure of prophetic utterance, the lines are divided so as to show the parallelism,
and strophes so as to show the refrain. Passages which
appear to be redactional additions are printed in smaller
type. The place of such as are simply removed to other
contexts is marked by * * * . Some footnotes were
naturally found indispensable, besides these typographical devices — not so much to justify the reconstruction
in detail, as to indicate in a general way on what theory
the critic has proceeded in his attempt to reproduce syn-
thetically all that remains of the discourse in its true
historical setting and original context. Also a marginal
reference or two is given where close correspondence in
thought or phraseology gives evidence of coinage from
the same mental mould. This mould may sometimes be
the evangelist's, sometimes (*e.g.* in case of the phrase,
"they have received their reward," in Mt. 6: 2, 5, 16,
compared with Lk. 6 : 24 and 16 : 25) we must at least
carry it back to some proto-evangelist behind our Matthew and our Luke, if not to Jesus himself. But justification in detail of every reading and every synthesis
adopted must not be expected. Let the results given be
rather regarded only as tentative suggestions, to stand or
fall according to subsequent developments. A heavy-
faced type has been employed for passages improperly
placed in the Sermon on the Mount and here restored to
their original connection, that the reader's attention may
be called to the fact.

Avoid Heathenish Patter

Mt. 6 : 7

Mt. 6 ⁷When ye pray, babble not by rote, as do the heathen, for they imagine they will be heard for their volubility. ⁸ * * * .
⁹ After this manner, therefore, pray ye : —

The Lord's Prayer

Lk. 11 : 2–4 = Mt. 6 : 9–13

Lk. 11 ² (i)   Father, hallowed be thy name ;
    (ii)   thy kingdom come
    (iii) ³ Daily give us our bread for the morrow.
    (iv) ⁴ And forgive us our sins, for we ourselves also forgive every debtor of ours.ᵃ *
    (v)   And bring us not into temptation.

ᵃ Mt. 18 : 35 ; Mk. 11 : 26.

* On the significance of the smaller type, see preceding note. The original form of the prayer would seem to have included simply five brief petitions. Hence the supporting clause attached to the petition for forgiveness will not have more valid claims to originality than the similar clauses appended in the Matthæan version to petitions ii and v, though the addition to petition iv is doubtless older, since it appears in both Matthew and Luke.

Parable of the Importunate Widow

Lk. 18 : 1–8

Lk. 18 ¹ And he spake a parable unto them on the need of always praying and never losing heart, saying,

> ² There was in a certain city a judge who had neither fear for God nor respect for man.   ³ And there was a widow in that city, and she came and said to him, Give me justice of my adversary.   ⁴ And for a time he would not.   But afterward he said to himself, Though I have no fear for God nor respect for man, ⁵ yet because this widow annoys me I will do her justice, that she may not plague me by her perpetual coming.   And the Lord said,ᵃ Hear what the unjust judge saith.   ⁷ And shall not God do justice for his own chosen people, who cry unto him day and night, though he be longsuffering in their case ? ⁸ I tell you he will vindicate them speedily. Yet when the Son of Man comes will he find faith on earth ? *

ᵃ Lk. 16 : 8.

* This parable is employed in the connection given it by Luke to support the doctrine of the nearness of "the day when the Son of Man is revealed" (17 : 30). But clearly the Parousia is here referred to only as an example of answers to prayer that seem long deferred, the principal aim being not to warn of the Parousia, but

Parable of the Importunate Friend

Lk. 11 : 5-8

Lk. 11 [5] And he said unto them : —

Which of you shall have a friend, and shall
go to him at midnight and say to him,
[6] Friend, lend me three loaves; for a friend
of mine has come to my house from a
journey, and I have nothing to set before
him; — [7] and he from inside shall answer
and say, Trouble me not: the door is now
shut and the children are with me in bed;
I cannot rise and give thee. [8] I tell you,
though he will not rise and give him anything because he is his friend, yet because
of his persistence he will get up and give
him all he requires.

Persist in Prayer

Lk. 11 : 9-13 = Mt. 7 : 7-11

Lk. 11 [9] And I tell you,

Ask, and it shall be given you,

Seek, and ye shall find,

Knock, and it shall be opened unto you.

to inculcate persistence in believing prayer (note v. 8[b]).
Accordingly we range this parable alongside its counterpart, the parable of the Importunate Friend, disregarding
the order of Luke. Both these parables fail to appear
in Matthew, perhaps because of the seemingly disparag-
ing comparison of the divine motive in hearing prayer.

[10] For everyone that asketh receiveth,
　　And he that seeketh findeth,
　　　　And to him that knocketh it shall be
　　　　opened.

Mt.　7　[9] Or what father of you, if his son ask
　　　　　bread will give him a stone ?
　　　　　[10] Or if he ask a fish, will he give him
　　　　　a serpent ?
Lk.　11　[13] If ye then, wicked as ye are, know
　　　　　how to give good gifts to your
　　　　　children,
　　　　　　how much more will your Father in
　　　　　heaven give good things to them
　　　　　that ask him ?

II. The Discourse on Earthly *vs.* Heavenly Wealth

Lk. 12 : 13–34; 16 : 1–9, 11–13 = Mt. 6 : 19–21, 24–34

The Occasion

Lk. 12 : 13–14

Lk. 12　[13] And a man from out the crowd said to him, Teacher, tell my brother to divide the inheritance with me.　[14] But he said to him, Man, who made me a judge or arbitrator over you ?

The Principle: Jesus shows what are the Real Values of Life

Lk. 12:15

Lk. 12 ¹⁵ And he said unto them,

Take heed and guard yourselves from all covetousness, for a man's living does not consist in his wealth — the things that he possesses.*

a v. 22;
Mt. 6:25.

Parable of the Rich Fool

Lk. 12:16-21

Lk. 12 ¹⁶ And he spake a parable unto them, saying,

A certain rich man's farm bore great crops. ¹⁷And he was reasoning with himself, saying, What shall I do, for I have no room to gather in my crops ? ¹⁸ And he said, This will I do. I will tear down my barns and build greater,* and will gather in thither all my grain and my produce. ¹⁹ And I will say to my soul, Soul, thou hast many goods laid up for many years ; take a rest, eat, drink and be merry. ²⁰ But God said unto him, Senseless man, this very night thy life will be required of thee ; who then will have all that thou hast prepared ? ²¹ So is he that storeth up for himself and is not rich as toward God.

b v. 24;
Mt. 6:26.

Application: Jesus shows that Life is not for Food and Raiment

Lk. 12 : 22–34 = Mt. 6 : 25–34

Lk. 12 ²² And he said unto his disciples,

Mt. 6 ²⁵ Therefore I tell you

Be not anxious as to your life what to eat,

Nor as to the body, what to put on.

Is not life more than food,

a Lk. 12 : 15, 22.

and the body than raiment ? ^{*a*}

²⁶ Consider the ravens,

how they sow not, nor reap,

nor do they garner into barns ;

yet God feedeth them.

Are not you worth more than they ?

²⁷ Which of you can add a span to his age by anxiety ?

²⁸ Why then be anxious about raiment ?

Take a lesson from the meadow-lilies' growth,

they toil not, neither do they spin ;

²⁹ Yet I tell you, Solomon himself, in all his splendor,^{*b*}

b Lk. 12 : 18, 19.
Eccl. 2 : 1–11.

was not robed like one of these.

³⁰ But if the meadow-grass, that is to-day

and to-morrow serves as fuel for the oven,

> God doth so clothe,
> shall he not much more clothe you,
>   distrustful ones ?
> [31] Take then no anxious thought,
>   saying, What shall we eat, or drink,
>   or wear ?
> [32] For all such things are the pursuit
>   of Gentiles ;
> but your Father knoweth ye need
>   all these things.*
> Seek ye then his kingdom ;
> and all these things shall be given
>   you besides.

Lk. 12 [32] Fear not, little flock,
> it is your Father's decree
> to give you the kingdom.

Mt. 6 [19] Lay up for yourselves no stores upon
>   earth
> where moth and rust consume
> and where thieves break in and steal.

---

* That is, those who are conscious of a divine calling, like Israel, the people of God, should assume that provision will be made for their needs at least equal to that made for ravens and lilies. The Gentiles have no such consciousness. Compare *Ps. Aristeas*, 140 (90 B.C.), "The Jews are called by the Egyptians the People of God, because they are not, like others, men of food and drink and clothing, but are given to searching out God's works."

Lk. 12 ³³Sell what ye have and give it for
alms,

make yourselves purses that do not
wear out,

a treasure in heaven that will not
fail,

Mt. 6 ²⁰where neither moth nor rust con-
sumes

and where thieves do not break in
nor steal.

²¹For where the treasure is, there also is
the heart.

Two Parables on the Use to be made of Earthly Wealth

*First Parable : Jesus shows by the Example of
the Provident Steward how Treasure can be
stored in Heaven*

Lk. 16 : 1–9

Lk. 16 ¹He said also unto the disciples,

There was a certain rich man who had a
steward, and accusation was brought him
against the steward of squandering his property. ²So he called him, and said to him,
What is this I hear about thee? Give in
the account of thy stewardship, for thou
mayst no longer be steward. ³Now the

steward said to himself, What am I to do,
seeing my master taketh away the stewardship from me? To dig I have not strength.
To beg I am ashamed. — ⁴ I know what
I will do, so that when I am put out of
the stewardship people may take me in to
their own homes. ⁵ So calling in each of
his master's debtors, he proceeded to say
to the first, How much owest thou to my
master? And he said, A hundred casks of
oil. And he said to him, Here ; take thy
contract, sit down at once and write fifty
instead. ⁷ Then he said to another, And
how much owest thou? And he said, A
hundred quarters of wheat. He says to
him, Take thy contract and write eighty.
⁸ And the master praised the dishonest
steward for his shrewd dealing ; for the
sons of this world are shrewder than the
sons of light in their conduct toward their
own generation. ⁹ And I tell you, Use your
' vile lucre ' to make friends for yourselves ;
so that when it fails, these may receive you
into eternal dwellings.*

* On the reasons for connecting Lk. 12 : 13-34 with
16 : 1-9, 11-13, see Appendix A (8), p. 154. We para-
phrase the peculiar expression " mammon of unrighteousness " (see below, Lk. 16 : 13, and cf. "steward of unrighteousness," v. 8, "judge of unrighteousness," Lk.
18 : 6) by the current phrase ' vile lucre.'

*Second Parable : Jesus shows by the Example of
the Intrusted Talents that God requires us to
turn our Resources and Opportunity to Good
Account*

Lk. 19 : 11–28 = Mt. 25 : 14–30

Lk. 19 ¹¹ And as they were listening to this,
he related to them a second parable, because he
was near Jerusalem, and they supposed the kingdom
of God was about to appear at once.* So he said,

* In the Lucan form the Parable of the Talents (Minæ)
has undergone a decided transformation, to which the
explanatory addition in 19 : 11 affords the key. The didactic intent of the parable is clearly man's responsibility
for God-given talent and opportunity. The mere length
of time to elapse before the accounting is not an essential
feature. Its purpose is therefore incorrectly stated in
Lk. 19 : 11. In Mt. 25 : 19 the "long time" simply al-
lows for the doubling of the intrusted capital. But take
just the features which appear only in the Lucan form
("to receive a kingdom and to return" in v. 12, verse 14,
"having received the kingdom" in v. 15, and verse 27),
and all subserve the purpose of making this change in
the original purpose. Not God but Christ now appears
as furnishing the capital, which is correspondingly reduced (twenty dollars as against fifty thousand) and
equally divided. (Nevertheless in v. 24 the first servant is still designated "He that had the ten minæ,"
implying an original in which the division, as in Matthew, had been *un*equal.) He goes *to receive a king-*

Mt. 25 [14] A certain man going on a journey summoned his slaves, and delivered to them his property. [15] To one he gave fifty thousand dollars, to another twenty, to another ten ; to each according to his ability. And he said to them, Do business with this till I return, and went away. [16] Straightway he

dom ; he is *opposed by his fellow-countrymen ;* he *returns to punish the rebellious.* All these new traits serve to transform the parable into an allegory of the Second Coming and echo the idea that it was uttered " Because he was nigh to Jerusalem and they supposed that the kingdom of God would immediately appear," an idea which the evangelist in other passages shows a desire to correct (*e.g.* 17 : 25). Moreover, besides the evidence of alteration in verse 24, all these new traits are drawn from the well-known experience of Archelaus (Jos. *Ant.* xvii, 9 : 3; 11 : 1–14; 13 : 1). The Lucan form is therefore certainly less original than the Matthæan, which we adopt. This, however, does not guarantee every detail of the Matthæan. Thus the last clause of verses 21 and 23 (wanting in the Lucan form) and verse 30 (composed of two refrains repeated in Mt. 8 : 12; 22 : 13; 25 : 30 and 8 : 12; 13 : 42, 50; 22 : 13; 24 : 51; 25 : 30) form an incongruous and probably later element. (See next note.) Luke, on the other hand, has a saying in 12 : 47–48 which should probably be added. For the servant who knew his Lord's will and did it not (a scarcely veiled reference to Israel, cf. Rom. 2 : 17–20 and Amos 3 : 1–2) is clearly the " unprofitable servant " of the parable. Here too the moral is, Superior opportunity implies greater responsibility.

o

that had received the fifty thousand dollars engaged in business with it and made fifty thousand more. [17] Likewise he of the twenty thousand, twenty thousand more. [18] But he that received the ten thousand went away and dug a hole in the ground and hid his master's money. [19] Now after a long time the master of those slaves comes and settles his account with them. [20] So he that had received the fifty thousand dollars came and brought fifty thousand more, saying, Sir, thou didst deliver to me fifty thousand dollars. See, I have gained fifty thousand more. [21] His master said unto him, Well done, good and faithful slave, thou wast faithful over few things, I will set thee over many. Enter thy master's feast.* [22] He also who had received the twenty thousand dollars came and said, Sir, thou deliveredst to me twenty thousand dollars. See, I have gained twenty thousand more. [23] His master said to him, Well done, good and faithful slave, thou hast been faithful over a few things, I will set thee over many. Enter thy master's feast.* [24] Then he who had received

---

* An assimilation by the evangelist of this parable to those he has placed alongside. The original has no reference to a feast, but suitably rewards the slave by a position of more exalted service.

the ten thousand came and said, Sir, I knew
thee to be an exacting man, reaping where
thou didst not sow, and garnering where
thou didst not winnow. [25]So I was afraid
and went and hid thy ten thousand dollars
in the ground. Here thou hast what belongs to thee. [26] But his master answering
said to him, Thou wicked and backward
slave ! Thou knewest that I reap where I
sowed not, and garner in where I winnowed
not? [27]Then oughtest thou to have placed
my money with the bankers, and I would
have gone and obtained my own with interest. [28] Therefore take away from him the
ten thousand dollars and give it to him that
hath the fifty thousand. Lk. 19 [28] I tell you,
To everyone that hath shall be given more,
and from him that hath not shall be taken
what he hath.

*First Application: Jesus teaches that the Use of
Wealth may show Fitness for Higher Things*

Lk. 16 : 10–13 = Mt. 6 : 24

Lk. 16 [10] He that is faithful in a very little is
faithful also in much,
and he that is faithless in a very
little is faithless also in much.

16 [11] If then ye were not found faithful in
the matter of vile lucre,
who will intrust to you the true
wealth?
[12] And if ye were not found faithful in
another's property,
who will give you your own?

[13] No house-servant can be slave to two
masters ;
for either he will hate the one and
love the other,
or else he will cling to one and hold
the other in aversion.
Ye cannot serve both God and Mammon.

*Second Application : Israel's Greater Enlighten-
ment implies Heavier Punishment for Unfaith-
fulness*
Lk. 12 : 47-48

Lk. 12 [47] Moreover that slave which knew his
master's will,[a]
yet made not ready nor did according to his will,
shall be beaten with many stripes.[b]
[48] But he that knew it not,
and did things worthy of stripes
shall be beaten with few.

[a] Rom. 2:17-
20.

[b] Am. 3:2.

> To whomsoever much is given,
> from him shall much be required,
> and with whomsoever people place
> much in trust,
> from him they demand the more.

Two Additional Parables on False Standards of Judgment

Occasion

Lk. 16: 14-15

Lk. 16 ¹⁴ Now the Pharisees were hearkening to all these things, they were avaricious,* and they began to mock at him. ¹⁵ And he said to them,

---

* If avarice was a sin specially characteristic of the Pharisees, of which we have no evidence elsewhere, it is not the one rebuked by Jesus in the words which follow, nor even in the ensuing parable of the Rich Man and Lazarus. Doubtless the early Christian opponent of the Pharisees saw his antagonist depicted in the person of Dives, and, as we shall see, found occasion even to extend the application of this minatory parable to the Jewish adherent of Moses and the Prophets by an addendum directed against Dives' "five brethren." But the parable itself does not call the rich man a Pharisee. It is not directed against love of money; but rebukes *worldly standards of judgment.* Its theme is precisely as stated in v. 15, "That which is exalted among men is an abomination in the sight of God." Men admire and

Ye are they that make yourselves out righteous in the sight of men [a] ; but God know-
eth your hearts.   For that which among

envy the rich man ; God may exalt the lowest beggar.
It does not belong to the exposition of this principle to
say that the rich man was bad and the beggar good, or
that he was a Pharisee and the beggar a Publican ; the
point, and the whole point, is that differences in earthly
conditions are not a blind to the divine judgment.   Thus
the clause, φιλάργυροι ὑπάρχοντες, in v. 14, and v. 15 *b*
are reciprocally exclusive ; and of the two alternative in-
timations, the saying of Jesus in v. 15 is as certainly correct as the editorial comment in v. 14 is incorrect, and
therefore appears in small type.   It is true, as we shall
see in the note next following, that the parable against
judging by worldly station would hardly be a rebuke
of the Pharisees if it stood alone.   It might almost represent the very feeling of the Pharisee himself toward
his great antagonist, the rich and worldly Sadducee.
But we have reason to think it did not stand alone, but
side by side with one as exactly fitted to v. 15 *a* as this
to 15 *b*.   And the full significance of both appears when
we bring in, as we have done, Lk. 12 : 47–48 in place of
16 : 13.   For now the reason for the scoffing of the Pharisees, so incomprehensible before, becomes apparent.   The
Pharisee's confidence was far from being in his riches —
rather the contrary — but in the fact of his " knowing his
Lord's will."   The scoffs were provoked by the threat of
" many stripes " for the servant who " knew his lord's will
and did it not," as compared with the few stripes of the

men is exalted is an abomination in the sight of God.*

am haaretz in his ignorance of the law. The real issue accordingly was broader than merely the superiority of the divine judgment to worldly conditions of wealth *vs.* poverty: this only led up to the more fundamental principle as stated in v. 15 and exemplified in the second parable, wherein the divine judgment is also shown to be superior to worldly (Pharisaic) estimates of *moral* worth.

* The very phraseology of 18: 9–14, a parable said to have been uttered " against certain who esteemed themselves to be righteous and despised others," but without any indication whatever of the occasion or provocation, is enough to show that it must have followed originally upon 16: 15. The very verb δικαιοῦν, common to 16: 15 and 18: 14 occurs nowhere else in the gospels in this sense save Mt. 12: 37, and, as we have seen (see preceding note), the context as imperatively demands teaching against this self-exaltation of the Pharisees. As the parable of the Rich Man and Lazarus shows how God " looks not upon the outward man, but upon the heart " in the case of worldly station, so its companion, the parable of the Pharisee and the Publican, applies the same principle to Pharisaic self-esteem. The τινές of 18: 9 had of course to be substituted for an original τούς, or πρὸς αυτοὺς διὰ τὸ πεποιθ., or the like, when the parable lost its original connection with 16: 14–15. That which now follows at this point, 16: 16–18, is clearly remote from the subject and easily demonstrated to belong in a different context (cf. Mt. 11: 12–13; 5: 18, 32, and see Appendix A (6)).

Parable of the Rich Man and the Beggar : Jesus teaches the Worthlessness of Human Standards of Respect

Lk. 16 : 19-25 [26-31]

Lk. 16 [19] Now there was a certain rich man, who was robed in purple and fine linen, and lived in splendid luxury every day. [20] And a certain pauper named Lazarus* lay at his gateway, [21] a mass of ulcers, and fain to eat the remnants from the rich man's table ; the very dogs would come and lick his ulcers. [22] In course of time the pauper died, and he was borne by the angels into the bosom of Abraham. And the rich man also died, and was entombed. [23] And in the underworld he lifted up his eyes, for he was one that was in torment, and sees afar off Abraham, and Lazarus in his bosom. [24] And calling aloud he said, Father Abraham, pity me, and send Lazarus to dip but the tip of his finger in water and cool my tongue, for I am in agony in this flame. [25] But Abraham said, My son, remember that thou didst receive thy good things to the full,[a] and in like manner Lazarus his evil things ; but now he is comforted here,

[1] Lk. 6 : 24 ; Mt. 6 : 2, 5, 16.

* *I.e.* Gotthelf — God help.

whereas thou art tormented. [26] And besides
all this a great chasm has been fixed between us and
you, so that those who might wish to cross hence
unto you are not able, nor can any cross from
thence unto us. [27] And he said, I entreat thee,
father, to send him to my father's house — [28] for I
have five brothers — that he may bear witness to
them, that they also may not come into this place
of torment. [29] But Abraham saith, They have
Moses and the prophets ; let them listen to them.
[80] But he said, Nay, father Abraham, but if someone
should go to them from the dead they would re-
pent. [31] But he answered him, If they harken not
to Moses and the prophets, they would not yield
were one even to rise from the dead.*

*Parable of the Pharisee and the Publican : Jesus
teaches who has Righteousness in God's Sight*

Lk. 18 : 9–14 (duplicate of v. 14 in Lk. 14 : 11) = Mt.
23 : 12

Lk. 18 [9] And he spake this parable against
such as put trust in themselves that they were
righteous and despised others : —

* The addition, ver. 26–31, introduces a theme alien
to the parable. Moreover it is borrowed from current
apocalyptic expectation, which taught that Moses and
Elias (sometimes Enoch and Elias, or Elias alone, Rev.
11 : 3–12 ; Mk. 9 : 11-13) would rise from the dead to
"witness" for Messiah, and turn Israel to him in repentance. See the article in the *Am. Journ. of Theol.*
above referred to (Appendix A, p. 155).

¹⁰ Two men went up into the temple to pray, the one a Pharisee and the other a Publican. ¹¹ The Pharisee stood and prayed after this style : O God, I thank thee that I am not like the rest of men, plunderers, dishonest, adulterers, or even like this Publican. ¹² I fast two days in the week. I pay tithes on every article I possess. ¹³ The Publican, standing afar off, would not so much as lift up his eyes to heaven, but beat upon his breast, saying, O God, be merciful to me, sinner that I am. ¹⁴ I tell you this man went to his home blessed with righteousness rather than the other.

For he that exalteth himself shall be humbled,

but he that humbleth himself shall be exalted.

III. First Discourse of the Crisis and Rejection in Galilee.* Jesus defends his Mission against the Covert Slander of the Scribes who came down from Jerusalem

Occasion

After feeding a multitude in the wilderness Jesus heals the dumb and blind, evoking Mes-

* The greater discourses of the period of Galilean activity, such as the Parables of the Kingdom, Mt. 13: 1–52,

sianistic acclamation, Mk. 8:1–10, 22ᵇ–26;
7:32–37 = Mt. 15:(29–31) 32–39; 9:27–34 =

do not appear to have been drawn upon by our first
evangelist for the filling up of the Sermon on the Mount.
One saying, Mt. 7:6, appears indeed to be more likely
to have been uttered in connection with the discourse to
the Twelve when sent to preach in Galilee, Mt. 9:35–
10:1 = Mk. 6:6–7 = Lk. 9:1–2 (*duplicate* 10:1–2);
Mt. 10:5–8; Mt. 10:9–11 = Mk. 6:8–10 = Lk. 9:3–4
(*duplicate* 10:4ᵃ); Mt. 10:12–13 = Lk. 10:4ᵇ–6; Mt.
10:14–15 = Lk. 10:10–12 (*duplicate* Lk. 9:5 = Mk.
6:11); Mk. 6:12 = Lk. 9:6. It might have been
uttered after Mt. 10:12–13 = Lk. 10:4ᵇ–6 with greater
probability than on occasion of Mt. 16:20, as proposed
by O. Holtzmann (*Leben Jesu*, p. 258). But the *logion*
was doubtless taken up by the evangelist from floating
tradition, and the attempt to fix on its original context is
altogether too precarious. The case is different with the
great discourse of Jesus' conflict in Capernaum with the
religious authorities, provoked by their blasphemous explanation of his miracles. As to this, the principal difficulties come rather from the multitude of independent
reports. It is quite clear, however, from the main accounts in Lk. 11:14–12:1 = Mt. 12:22–50 that we have
two principal discourses to distinguish, (1) that of the
morning, when, arriving home from the scene of culmination of his popularity, Jesus finds the scribes from
Jerusalem in possession of the field, and himself put upon
the defensive by the slander covertly (Mt. 12:25 = Lk.
11:17) set in circulation by them, " He exorciseth by
Beelzebub." The discourse of the morning is accord-

John 9 : 1–6 ; 10 : 19–20 (*duplicate* Mk. 6 : 30–
56 = Mt. 14 : 13–36 = Lk. 9 : 10–17 = John
6 : 1–21) ; Mt. 12 : 22–23 = Lk. 11 : 14. These
murmurs of popular approval are met on the
part of certain scribes who had come down from
Jerusalem by the verdict, He casteth out devils
by Beelzebub, Mk. 3 : 22 = Mt. 12 : 23^{b}–24
(*duplicate* 9 : 34) = Lk. 11 : 15 = John 10 : 21.*

ingly defensive. But (2) at the noonday meal, Lk.
11 : 37–41 = Mk. 7 : 1–21, the scribes from Jerusalem
and their Pharisaic adherents found occasion for a direct
attack, and openly charged him with neglect of the ordinances of ceremonial cleanness. Jesus then takes up
the gauntlet, publicly renounces ceremonialism, and
formally turns the accusation back upon his accusers by
denouncing prophetic woes against Pharisees and scribes
alike. To their demand of a sign from Heaven in authentication of these revolutionary utterances he replies
(3) with the offer of the sign of Jonah and the Ninevites,
Solomon and the Queen of Sheba. These two later discourses, in which Jesus takes the offensive, may therefore be more appropriately treated as separate, although
their connection with the first in both occasion and content is intimate.

* As I have shown in my *Introduction* (p. 207), at
least this portion of Mark contains duplicate material,
which naturally causes still further duplication when it
reappears in the dependent gospel of Matthew. Luke
is characteristically more cautious and omits the more

(1) *Feeding of the Multitude*

Mk. 8 : 1–10 = Mt. 15 : 32–39 (*duplicate*, Mk. 6 : 30–56
    = Mt. 14 : 13–36 = Lk. 9 : 10–17 = Jn. 6 : 1–21)

Mk. 8 [1] In those days, when there was again[a] a   [a] 6 : 34.
great multitude and they had nothing to eat, he
called his disciples and saith to them, [2] I have
compassion on the multitude, because it is now
three days that they have been staying with me,
and they have nothing to eat. [3] And if I send
them away to their homes fasting, they will faint
by the way; and some of them are come from
far. [4] And the disciples answered him, Whence
could one supply these men with bread here in
the wilderness? [5] And he asked them, How
many loaves have ye? And they said, Seven.
[6] And he bade the multitude be seated on the
ground. And he took the seven loaves and
gave the thanksgiving and brake, and gave to
his disciples to set before them, and they set it

glaring instances, such as the two feedings of the multitude and two collisions with the scribes from Jerusalem,
though not all duplication is avoided (Lk. 8 : 19–21 =
11 : 27–28). The fourth gospel is as usual controlled by
the third. In our text the simpler and more original form
is of course made the basis. In Mk. 8 : 1 it contains
the single word, πάλιν, "again," from the editorial pen.

before the multitude. ⁷And they had a few little fish, and he blessed them and bade distribute these also. ⁸And they ate and were filled. And they took up seven baskets of fragments that were left over. ⁹Now there were about four thousand of them.

ᵃ Mk. 6:45. And he dismissed them,ᵃ ¹⁰and straightway, entering into the boat with his disciples, came into the parts of Dalmanutha.*

(2) *Healing a Blind Man by touching his Eyes with Spittle*

Mk. 8:22ᵇ–26 = Mt. 9:27–31 (*duplicates* in 12:22; 20:30–34) = Jn. 9:1–12

Mk. 8 ²²* * *† And they bring unto him a
ᵇ v. 32. blind man,ᵇ and entreat him to touch him.ᵇ

* For Dalmanutha Matthew has Magadan. The places are unknown, but either name designates some obscure place on the shore of the Gennesaret plain, not far from Capernaum. The duplicate account in Mk. 6:53 has "came to land at Gennesaret, and moored to the shore." They had been driven from their intended course to Bethsaida (6:45) by a strong headwind from the northeast (the usual direction of violent winds on the lake), and thus landed probably somewhere along the southern extremity of the plain.

† The first clause of Mk. 8:22 should be reckoned with the preceding context. The healing of the blind

[23] And he took hold of the blind man with his hand and led him forth outside the village,[a] and when he had spat upon his eyes[b] and laid his hands on him[c] he asked him if he saw anything. [24] And he looked up and said, I see men ; for I

a v. 33.
b v. 33;
Jn. 9:6.
c v. 33.

man is an incident so thoroughly marked and so closely connected with that of Mk. 7 : 32–37 as to compel identification with that which both in Mt. 9 : 27–34 and Mt. 12 : 22 is associated with the casting out of the dumb devil. Why it was removed from this connection in Mark to one which locates it at Bethsaida can only be conjectured. That the location is incorrect is apparent from verses 23 and 26, where the locality is called a κώμη, *i.e.* "village" or "hamlet." Jn. 9 : 1–12 locates this healing at Jerusalem, with a mystical reference to the pool of Siloam (cf. ἀπέστειλεν, v. 25). This is of course still more incompatible with the κώμη of Mark. That the incident is really the same is evidenced not merely by the remarkable trait of the use of spittle (cf. also Mk. 7 : 33), but (1) by the altercation with the Pharisees on spiritual blindness, which follows in Jn. 9 : 35–41, culminating in v. 41 with the declaration on Jesus' part that the sin of the Pharisees is eternal, and (2) by the calumny on their part, "He hath a devil," 10 : 20. On the authority of so many cases where a healing of the blind is connected with the altercation with the Pharisees (Mt. 9 : 27–34 ; 12 : 22–32 ; 15 : 30–16 : 1 ; Jn. 9 : 1–10 : 21 ; see also Lk. 11 : 34–36 and Mt. 15 : 14) we venture to transpose Mk. 8 : 22[b]–26 to a position immediately before 7 : 32–37.

behold as it were trees * walking about. ²⁵Then
he put his hands again upon his eyes,^a and he
looked and was restored, and saw all things
clearly. ²⁶And he sent him away^b to his house,
saying, Do not even enter the village.

^a 9: 27.

^b Jn. 9:7.

(3) *Healing of a Dumb Man, followed by Popular Acclamation*

Mk. 7: 32–37 = Mt. 9: 32–33 (*duplicate* [Mk. 6: 53–56]
Mt. 12 : 22–23^a = Lk. 11 : 14 = Jn. 6 : 14)

^c v. 22.

^d v. 22.

^e v. 23.

^f v. 23.

^g v. 23;
Jn. 9:6.

^h 5:41.

Mk. 7 ³²And they bring unto him^c one that
was dumb and had an impediment of speech,
^dand entreat him to lay his hand on him.
^{33 e}And he took him aside apart from the crowd
by himself, and put his fingers in his ears,^f and
spat and touched his tongue^g. ³⁴And looking
up to heaven he sighed, and saith to him,
Ephphatha,^h that is, Be opened. ³⁵And his ears
were opened and straightway the bond of his
tongue was loosed, and he spoke rightly. ³⁶And

* The trunk of a tree — the blind do not consider the
top — compares closely in dimensions with a human
body. This blind man realizes that the moving objects
of this size must of course be men. Compare the inter-
esting description of the gradual restoration of speech
to the dumb man immediately following.

he charged them to tell no man. But the more
he charged them the more exceedingly did they
proclaim the matter.[a] And people were aston-
ished beyond all measure, saying, [37] He hath
done all things well, he maketh even the deaf to
hear and the dumb to speak.[b] *

a 1 : 44–45.

b Mt. 9 : 33;
12 : 23;
15 : 30–31;
Lk. 11 : 14;
Jn. 6 : 14.

* The identification of the two healings of the blind
and dumb in the two passages of Mark above given, with
the casting out of a "dumb devil" in Lk. 11 : 14, the
healing of two blind and one dumb in Mt. 9 : 27–33, and
of one "blind and dumb" in Mt. 12 : 23, may seem to
require more than has thus far been adduced to justify
it ; especially if we proceed so far as to make the healing of the blind in Jn. 9 : 1–10 : 21 refer to the same.

One of the principal notes of identity is the special
notice of the amazement of the multitude which in this
case is carried to the highest pitch of all the Markan
narratives (cf. 2 : 12 ; 5 : 42) ; not of course that the
miracle is more surprising than the raising of Jairus'
daughter, but that the evangelist would describe it as
the actual culmination of popular wonder which precipitated a momentous conflict. For, to take up at once a
second and third note of identity, the narrative proceeds
to relate (2) the Feeding of the Multitude, and the
effort of the Pharisees to counteract Jesus' popularity by
attributing his miracles to Satan (a trait wanting in Mk.
8 : 11), and (3) demanding a sign from Heaven. In
like manner Lk. 11 : 14, Mt. 9 : 32, and Mt. 12 : 24,
which add the blasphemy of the Pharisees, all proceed
from the amazement of the multitude to the demand of a

P

(4) *Messianistic Acclamation met by the Scribes from Jerusalem : 'He casteth out by Beelzebub'*

Mt. 12:23ᵇ–24 (*duplicate* 9: 34) = Mk. 3:22 = Lk. 11:15 = Jn. 10:20

Mt. 12 ²³And they said, Can this be the Son of David? ²⁴But when the Phari-

sign from Heaven, Mt. 12: 23 f. giving the distinctively Messianist character to the acclamation that the people said, " Is not this the Son of David." Now the only occasion of this kind we know of, an occasion which in its public features could hardly be repeated, is related in Jn. 6: 14–15, where again it leads to the demand of a sign from Heaven (v. 30–33), here also following upon the feeding of the multitude, yet not because of it, but because " the people saw the signs (true reading, cf. v. 2) which he did." This identification is clinched by the duplication of Mt. 12: 38–39 in Mt. 16: 1–5 = Mk. 8: 11–13. A fourth note of identity appears in the next succeeding item, a discourse of Jesus warning against the teaching of the Pharisees under the figure of bread, which is followed by the withdrawal to Cæsarea Philippi and Confession of Peter, Mk. 8 : 14–22ᵃ, 27–30 = Mt. 16: 5–12, 13–16. Of this Luke has but the brief statement 12 : 1, but John expands into the great discourse on the true Bread from Heaven with a curiously variant version of the Petrine Confession, 6 : 22–65, 66–71.

If these incidents be studied in their interrelation as a group, of which sometimes two or three, sometimes more, are always found together, the portions of Mark omitted by Luke, but which appear in Matthew, and by their ap-

sees* heard it, they said, this man only casteth
out devils by Beelzebub, the prince of the devils.

pearance give rise to the remarkable doublets of that
gospel, such as 12: 38–39 = 16: 1–5, will appear in their
true light. Mk. 8: 22ᵇ–26 (displaced as shown above,
p. 206 note †), 7: 32–37 are the two specific healings of
the blind and dumb, related in all the pristine freshness
and graphic detail of the Markan source, which in the
later accounts are more vaguely spoken of as healings of
two blind men and a dumb man (Mt. 9: 27–33 — Note
that the popular cry, " Is not this the Son of David," of
Mt. 12: 23, is here placed in the mouth of the healed
blind men with further assimilation to the Bartimæus
episode, Mt. 20: 30–34 = Mk. 10: 46–52), "one possessed with a devil, blind and dumb" (Mt. 12: 22), a
"dumb devil" (Lk. 11: 14 — Note, however, the connected saying on spiritual blindness, vv. 34–36), "a man
blind from birth " (Jn. 9: 1–10: 21), and "signs done on
them that were sick" (Jn. 6: 2). Everywhere the distinctive feature of these particular healings (or at least
of one of the two) is that they precipitated the great
crisis when the Pharisees on their part blasphemed
Jesus as possessed of an unclean spirit, took him openly
to task as "a sinner" (Mk. 7: 1–24 = Mt. 15: 1–20),
and demanded a sign from Heaven, Jesus replying by a
true Philippic against the Pharisees. If this fact receive
adequate consideration, it will at once appear why we
further include in our identification Jn. 9: 1–10: 21 ; cf.
9: 24, 40–41 ; 10: 20 with Mt. 12 : 24, 32.

* Mark : "the scribes who had come down from Jerusalem," cf. 7: 1.

Jesus' Defence

Mt. 12:25–32 (34, 36–37?) = Lk. 11:17–23; 12:10 =
Mk. 3:23–30 *

(1) *Is Satan's Kingdom divided?*

Mt. 12:25–26 = Mk. 3:23–26 = Lk. 11:17–18

Mt. 12 [25] And when he perceived their thoughts
he said unto them : —

> Every kingdom divided against itself be-
> cometh desolate
> and every city or household divided against
> itself is overthrown.

---

* In my *Introduction*, p. 209, I have endeavored to
show that the sparing use of the *Logia* in Mark is not
due to lack of acquaintance on the part of our second
evangelist with that primitive compilation, instancing
Mk. 1:15 as affected by Lk. 4:21 (cf. 6:1–6); 1:24 by
Mt. 8:29, from which Mark deduces the general theory
1:34; 3:11 f., and giving as examples of displaced *Logia*
fragments in Mark, 2:28; 4:22, 24[b]; 8:34 f., 38[a]; 9:37,
41–50; 10:11, 15, 38[b], 39[b]; 11:22–25; 12:38[b], 39;
13:9–13, 21–23, 33–37; 14:25 (?). To these must be
added 3:22–30, an extract — to judge from its less complete form and anachronistic position — from the source
employed in Mt. 12:22–32 (*duplicate* in 9:32–34) =
Lk. 11:14–22; 12:10. In Mark its position is prema-
ture (see B. Weiss, *Markusevang.*, ad loc.), as appears
from the reference to the delegation from Jerusalem
(7:1–2) in v. 22, and in v. 23 to the parabolic teaching
to which we are first introduced in 4:2. It appears to

²⁶ And if Satan is casting out Satan he is di-
    vided against himself;
  how then shall his kingdom stand?

be inserted at this point in the narrative to palliate the
sin of Jesus' mother and brethren, who came to lay hands
on Jesus, saying, " he is beside himself," a venial offence
of ignorance, by contrasting the " sin which hath never
forgiveness " of " the scribes from Jerusalem." But it is
the more inappropriate to a chronological narrative at
this point because the incident of the mother and brethren is itself already an unchronological appendix to the
section on the choosing of the Twelve, 3 : 7–15ᵃ, which has
first been supplemented by a list of the twelve names,
very awkwardly attached, next by the incident of the
mother and brethren, doubtless for the sake of the saying
3 : 34–35, on the disciples as spiritual brethren who take
the place of earthly kin, and finally by the contrasted incident of the blasphemy of the scribes, 3 : 22–30. At what
period in the unknown history of our second gospel this
intercalation was made is a difficult problem, but certainly
before it was utilized by either Matthew or Luke, since
both show its effect (cf. Mt. 12 : 46–50; Lk. 8 : 19–21).

It is not improbable that the series of events related
in Mk. 8 : 22ᵇ–26; 7 : 32–37; 8 : 1–10, 11–13, 14–21, since
it is so closely paralleled by 6 : 30–56; 7 : 1–31, 27–33,
and in the other gospels, may have once included the
substance of 3 : 22–30 between 8 : 10 and 11. As it is,
Mk. 3 : 22–30 is simply a third form of the Logian version more fully given in Matthew and Luke. The
Markan tradition only comes in independently for the
later discourses of the day.

(2) *By Whom do your Sons exorcise ?*

Mt. 12 : 27–28 = Lk. 11 : 19–20

27 And if I by Beelzebub cast out demons
by whom do your sons cast them out ;
[therefore let them be your judges ?]
28 But if I by the Spirit of God cast out demons
then has the kingdom of God come unto
you.

(3) *Taking the Spoil of the Strong Man armed*

Mt. 12 : 29 = Mk. 3 : 27 = Lk. 11 : 21–22

29 Or how can one enter a strong man's house
and carry off his possessions,
unless first he have bound the strong man,
and then he will carry off his household as
spoil.

(4) *Decide for Friendship or Enmity*

Mt. 12 : 30 = Lk. 11 : 23

30 He that is not with me is against me ;
and he that gathereth not with me scattereth.

(5) *Blasphemy of God's Spirit an Abiding Sin*

Mt. 12 : 31–32 = Mk. 3 : 28–30 = Lk. 12 : 10 =
Jn. 9 : 39–41

31 Therefore I declare unto you,
All (other) sin and blasphemy shall be forgiven unto men

but blasphemy of the Spirit shall not be forgiven.

[32] And whoso speaketh a word against the Son
of Man

it shall be forgiven him ;

but whoso speaketh against the Holy Spirit,

it shall neither be forgiven him in this world,

nor in that which is to come.

[33] * * * * * * * *

(6) *The Evil Word shall bring into Judgment*

Mt. 12 : 34, 36-37

[34] Ye brood of vipers, how can ye, evil as ye
are, speak good things?

For out of the overflowing of the heart the
mouth speaketh

[35] * * * * * * * †

[36] But I tell you that for every idle word that
men speak

---

* Verses 33 (" Make the tree good or evil ") and 35
(The good man bringing forth good) are duplicates of
Mt. 7 : 10 = Lk. 6 : 43 and of Lk. 6 : 45ᵃ respectively.
See Appendix A (10), p. 161–166, and compare Luke.
Their true place appears to be the Sermon on the Mount.

† See the preceding note. These added logia of Matthew 12 : 33–37 which do not appear in the parallels are
of decidedly doubtful originality in the connection, especially as they partake largely of the nature of current
maxims and show affinity with foreign material (with
34ᵃ cf. Mt. 3 : 7).

they shall render account in the day of
judgment.
[37] For by thy words thou shalt be justified
and by thy words thou shalt be condemned.

IV. Second Discourse of the Crisis and Rejection in Galilee. Jesus is taken to Task for Disregard of the Traditions, and openly breaks with Scribes and Pharisees

Occasion

At the midday meal in a Pharisee's house Jesus
and his disciples provoke attack by neglecting
the ablutions.

Lk. 11 : 37–38 = Mk. 7 : 1–5 = Mt. 15 : 1–2

Lk. 11 [37] Now as he was speaking a Pharisee asked him to take lunch at his house.
Mk. 7 [1] And the Pharisees gathered unto him,
and certain scribes which had come from Jerusalem.* [2] And seeing certain disciples of his to

* This delegation of scribes from Jerusalem was a
matter of no small importance. It is indeed only Mark
who appreciates this, these scribes in Matthew and Luke
being either altogether lost to sight behind the habitual
antagonists of Jesus, the Pharisees, as in Mt. 9 : 34;
12 : 24; Lk. 11 : 15, or losing their identity in the more
general expression of Mt. 15 : 1, "scribes and Pharisees"

be eating bread with common, that is unwashed
hands — [3] for the Pharisees and all the Jews will
(cf. 23 : 2, 13, 15); but the overwhelming effect of their
authoritative verdict on Jesus' following shows their importance. It was a particular visit to Galilee of certain
great Jerusalem authorities, and the attributing of the
miracles of Jesus to collusion with Satan was surely their
work, as Mark declares (3 : 22), although, as we have
seen, the separation of 3 : 22–30 from 7 : 1–24 is certainly
unchronological. As Mk. 7 : 1 is clearly the *first* mention of this delegation, and there are no traces of 3 : 22–
30 having been removed from chapter 7, it is probable
that this account (Mk. 6 : 30–7 : 31; 8 : 34–35; 9 : 2–10),
which passes directly from the Feeding of the Multitude
(5000) and Walking on the Sea to the controversy on
Neglect of the Ablutions, with only a general reference
to the Miracles of Healing (Matthew, however, emphasizing in particular "the blind and the dumb"), thence
to the Exile and Revelation of Peter, and is paralleled
by Mt. 14 : 13–15 : 29ᵇ; 10 : 32, 33, 39; 17 : 1–13, had no
account of the discourse of the morning. It is clearly a
Markan source of Petrine type, but may perhaps have
been known to Matthew in independent form, since the
Matthæan version adds important and sometimes apparently original traits (Mt. 14 : 28–31; 15 : 12–15, 23–25).
Luke's cancellations may perhaps be similarly accounted
for. But this account of the Crisis in Galilee is not the
only one employed by Mark, nor indeed would it seem
the more original. Let it be designated Mark B, and
alongside it we shall have Mark A, *i.e.* 8 : 22ᵇ–26; 7 : 32–
37; 8 : 1–22ᵃ, 27–38; 9 : 1, 11–13, a narrative which re-

not eat unless they have punctiliously (?) washed their hands, in observance of the tradition of the elders ; ⁴ and when they come from the market-place they will not eat without washing, and they have many other traditional observances, washings of cups and pans and kettles — ⁵ and the Pharisees and scribes ask him, Why do not thy disciples walk according to the tradition of the elders, but eat bread with unwashed hands?

Jesus' Reply and Counter-Accusation

(1) *The True Purification of Meats*

Lk. 11 : 39–41 = Mt. 23 : 25–26

Lk. 11 ³⁹ And the Lord said unto him * : —

Now do ye Pharisees purify the outside of cup and platter, but the inside of you† is

lates in more specific form the Healings of the Blind and Dumb, then the Feeding of the Multitude (4000), coming to Gennesaret and Conflict with the Pharisees, then the Flight and Exile and Revelation of Peter, but dwells upon other features. Both A and B have passed over into Matthew, practically without cancellation, but Luke and John exercise discrimination in different ways, by selection and cancellation of the more obvious duplicates.

* According to Luke it was the particular Pharisee who was Jesus' host that put the question.

† Text " of you." This is a manifest misunderstanding (occasioned perhaps by v. 44). It is the *dishes* (so

full of robbery and extortion. [40] Simpletons, did not he who made the outside
make the inside as well? [41] But give the
contents for alms, and lo, all things are
purified for you.

(2) *The Ordinances of the Scribes nullify the
Word of God*

Mk. 7 : 6–13 = Mt. 15 : 3–9

Mk. 7 [6] But he said unto them : —

Well did Isaiah prophesy regarding you
hypocrites, as it is written, "This people
honoreth me with their lips, but their heart
is far from me. [7] But in vain do they worship me, teaching as their doctrines the
ordinances of men." [8] Ye forsake the commandment of God, and hold to the tradition of men.

Matthew) which contain the robbery and wickedness
(Matthew, "extortion"), not the *men;* for the Semitic
idiom substitutes the abstract for the concrete, as in Am.
3 : 10, princes "who store up violence and robbery," *i.e.*
the *fruits* of violence and robbery, in their palaces. To
really purify this food the contents should be restored to
the poor in alms, as was done by Zacchæus, Lk. 19 : 8 ;
then what remained might be counted "pure." This is
a spiritualizing application of the ceremonial law characteristic not only of Jesus, but of the broader piety of men
of his class in this age (cf. Mk. 12 : 32).

⁹ And he said unto them : —

Full well do ye make void the commandment of God that ye may keep your own
tradition. ¹⁰ For Moses said, " Honor thy
father and thy mother," and, " He that
slandereth father or mother, let him surely
be put to death." ¹¹ But ye say : If a man
say to father or mother, Whatever income
you might have from my wages is *korban*,
that is, dedicated to the temple treasury,
¹² you do not allow him to do any more
work for his father or his mother, ¹³ thus
nullifying the word of God by your tradition which ye have handed down. And
there are many like things which ye do.

(3) *Jesus sweeps away All Distinctions of
Meats*

Mk. 7 : 14–23 = Mt. 15 : 10–20

Mk. 7 ¹⁴ And he called up again the multitude
and said to them : —

¹⁵ Hear me all of you and understand.
There is nothing from outside a man that
by passing into him can make him ' impure ' ; but it is the things that are from
within a man that make the man ' impure.'

¹⁷ Now when he had come into the house,
away from the multitude, his disciples asked

him the meaning of the parable. [18] And he saith to them, " Are you also such simpletons? [a]   Do you not perceive that nothing that enters into a man from without can make him impure? [19] Because it does not penetrate to his soul, but goes into his belly and is thrown off into the drain." He thus pronounced all kinds of food to be 'pure.' And he went on to say, " What makes the man impure is that which issues from him. [21] For it is from within, out of men's souls that come forth malicious designs, fornication, theft, murder, [22] adultery, concupiscence, wickedness, fraud, licentiousness, an evil eye,[b] blasphemy,[c] arrogance, folly. [23] All these wicked things come forth from within, and these make the man impure. " *

[a] Lk. 11 : 40.

[b] Lk. 11 : 34.

[c] Mk. 3 : 22.

* The explanation of the parable is introduced out of chronological order precisely as in Mk. 4 : 10–13, and with just the same formula. In fact later private explanation appears to be a special device of Mark (cf. 9 : 33 ; 10 : 10 ; 11 : 20). Accordingly our typographical system requires that this portion be printed in the same manner as the evangelist's explanations and comments, although it embodies words of Jesus, perhaps even an allusion (v. 22[b]) to the blasphemy of the scribes. But the principal discourse must be supposed to be resumed thereafter independently of the aside.

(4) *Jesus denounces Three Woes upon the Pharisees*

Lk. 11 : 42–44 = Mt. 23 : 23, 6–7 , 27–28 *

(i) ⁴²Woe to you Pharisees
because you pay tithes on mint and
rue and every garden herb
and pass by justice and the love of God.
These ye should have done, while ye
left not those undone.

(ii) ⁴³Woe to you Pharisees
because you love the place of honor in
the synagogues
and salutations in the market places.

(iii) ⁴⁴Woe to you
because you are like unmarked tombs†
and men that pass over them know it
not.

* Matthew incorrectly combines this *Denunciation
uttered to* the scribes and Pharisees with a much later
discourse of Jesus *to his disciples*, in which he warns
them against the *spirit of* the scribes and Pharisees, Mk.
12 : 38ᵃ, 40 = Mt. 23 : 1–3 = Lk. 20 : 45–47.   It is with
this latter that we should probably connect the fragment
from the Sermon on the Mount on How to Discriminate
between True and False Teachers, Mt. 7 : 15–16[20?] =
Lk. 6 : 44.   See Appendix A (10), p. 163.

† There seems to be a curious discrepancy in our two
reports of this saying.   Both Mt. 23 : 27 and Lk. 11 : 44

(5) *He turns his Threefold Invective upon the Scribes as well*

Lk. 11 : 45–47[48–51] = Mt. 23 : 4, 29–32, 14

Lk. 11 [45] And one of the scribes answered him and saith, Teacher, in saying these things thou art insulting even us. [46] But he said : —

  (i) Woe unto you scribes also ;
     because ye lade men with burdens heavy to bear
     and yourselves will not touch the burdens with one of your fingers.

  (ii) [47] Woe unto you
     because you build up tombs for the prophets

compare the Pharisees to the sepulchres, and allude to the custom of whitewashing them that the passer-by might not unwittingly be ceremonially contaminated. But in Matthew it is the *whited* sepulchre to which the Pharisee is compared, as " outwardly beautiful " (?) but inwardly loathsome ; to which it may well be objected that the object of the whitewashing was just the reverse of making them appear beautiful. In Luke it is the *un*-whited sepulchre, by which the unwary are defiled without knowing it. This paradoxical arraignment of the professional " Puritan " of the day as a really defiling influence is perhaps not too strong to be genuine, and on the whole preferable to the Matthæan form.

and your own fathers put them to
death.

⁴⁸ So you are witnesses for and give consent to
the works of your fathers, because they
killed them and you build their tombs.
⁴⁹ On account of this "The Wisdom of
God" also saith : —

Mt. 23 ³⁴ Behold, I send unto you prophets and
wise men and scribes.

Some of them ye will kill and crucify
and some of them ye will scourge in
your synagogues
and persecute from city to city.

³⁵ That all the righteous blood shed upon
the earth
may come on your heads,
from the blood of Abel the just
to the blood of Zacharias son of Bara-
chias
whom ye slew between the temple and
the altar.

³⁶ Of a truth I tell you,
All these things shall come upon this
generation.

³⁷ Jerusalem, Jerusalem,
thou that killest the prophets
and stonest them that are sent unto thee,
how often would I fain have gathered
thy children
as a hen doth gather her chickens under
her wings
and ye would not.

³⁸ Behold your house is left to you forsaken ;

[89] for I tell you ye shall not see me henceforth

until ye shall say, Blessed is he that
cometh in the name of the Lord.*

* This quotation from an unknown writing of the
Hoqmah (Wisdom) literature shows itself to be an editorial insertion by its interruption of the threefold woes
against the scribes, the scribes being rather, from its
point of view, one of the three types of messengers of
the divine Wisdom; for the Lucan form, " prophets and
apostles," is of course less original than the Matthæan
" prophets, wise-men and scribes." It is clear, too, that
the speaker in the fragment is, as Luke says, not Jesus,
but the Wisdom of God, which usually is the case in the
Wisdom Literature (Prov. 7–9). Personified as the redemptive agency of God she pleads with men, but pleads
in vain until the day of Messiah, when the house, forsaken
of God's presence now because of Israel's obduracy (cf.
I Esdr. 1 : 33), will be filled with his renewed presence
among a regenerate people. The adaptation of Ps. 91 : 4,
in v. 37, scarcely conceivable in the mouth of Jesus, is most
appropriate to Wisdom as the redemptive agency of God
(cf. Prov. 8 : 3–21). Still more may this be said of the
mournful announcement of withdrawal from the temple
until a time of repentant welcome, in vv. 38–39. It is only
the ecclesiastical identification of Jesus with the Wisdom
of God, early as this was (cf. I Cor. 1 : 24; 2 : 6–16), which
permitted the placing of this quotation in a direct sense
in the mouth of Jesus. In Luke fortunately the original
speaker is still unobscured, though the fragment is divided
between 11 : 49–51 and 13 : 34–35 and otherwise altered.

(iii) [52] Woe unto you scribes
        because ye have taken away the key of
            knowledge.
        Ye enter not in yourselves
        And them that would enter in ye hinder.

(6) *A Further Denunciation of Scribal Casuistry**

Mt. 23 : 15–22, 24

Mt. 23 [15] Woe unto you, scribes and Pharisees,
        hypocrites ;
        because ye make the circuit of sea
            and land to gain one proselyte,

---

* The number of *seven* woes made up by Matthew is clearly factitious, like his series of ten miracles in chapters 8–9, and seven parables in chapter 13, or the seven "signs" or seven "I am" parables of the fourth gospel. The six "woes" of Is. 5 : 8–24 need not have been in the mind either of Jesus or the evangelists, a threefold form is natural in itself and is repeatedly employed by Jesus, may even be called a favorite with him (*e.g.* Mt. 6 : 2–4, 5–6, 16–18 ; Mk. 9 : 43–48 ; Mt. 23 : 8–10), and in the Lucan version of the denunciation we see such a three-fold division, first three woes upon the Pharisees, then three more upon the scribes. The primary difference in the Matthæan form is in the obliteration of the distinction between such as were appropriate to the Pharisees, who did not "sit in Moses' seat" (Mt. 23 : 2), nor "bind heavy burdens" (v. 11), nor "take away the key of knowledge" (v. 13), since not they but the scribes were

and when he is won ye make him
twofold more a son of perdition
than yourselves.

the teachers; and such as were appropriate to the
scribes, who were not characterized by a punctilious
scrupulosity of performance such as characterized their
slavish pupils, the Pharisees. By lumping "scribes and
Pharisees" together in the general formula "scribes
and Pharisees, hypocrites," the double series of threes
becomes simply a sequence of six, which there was
strong temptation to expand to the favorite number
seven, as in the case of the parables (chapter 13).

But the process has been complicated in two ways.
(1) Instead of the first Lucan "woe" against the scribes
we find a reference to the Jewish propaganda in all
lands, whereas the material of the woe serves as an ep-
exegetical addition to the warning not to imitate the
scribes in their life (Mt. 23:3). The substitution is by
no means happy, but as to the source of the substitute,
v. 15, we have no clew. (2) To make up the desired
seven woes two different methods have been followed in
different texts. (*a*) Verses 16–22, which Blass brackets
in his edition of 1901, on the ground of omission by
Chrysostom and the internal evidence, are certainly no
part of the original denunciation, as appears both from the
introductory formula and from the strophic form; but
the evidence for excluding them from the canonical Matthew is very weak, and even the occasion of their original
utterance may have been the same. (*b*) Certain other
inferior authorities, either because the absence of verses
16–22 made the supply of a seventh woe seem necessary,

[16] Woe unto you, ye blind guides
which say, Whoso sweareth by the
sanctuary it is nothing,
But whoso sweareth by the gold of
the sanctuary is bound by his oath.
[17] Ye fools and blind ;
for which is greater, the gold, or the
sanctuary that made the gold holy?

or because the difference in the introductory formula seemed to exclude 16 ff. from the count, introduce verse 14, a "woe" made up from Mk. 12 : 40.

In a word the confusion produced by Matthew in the Galilean twofold triple denunciation seems to be due to the attempt to combine it with another discourse, or two other discourses, unknown outside of Mt. 23, the whole in combination being framed to produce a series of seven woes against the "hypocrites" of orthodox Judaism. Whether part of this foreign material came in, as Blass conjectures, subsequently to the publication of our canonical gospel, or whether, as our use of uniform type implies, our evangelist himself made the combination, omitting to conform the introductory formula of v. 16 to 13, 15, 23, 25, 27, and 29 only because he was not aiming at a series of seven, but only to reproduce the two threes of his model, is a subordinate question. The above, however, will represent the principal elements of fact in a discussion of The Seven Woes of Matthew's Gospel which has come to hand since this volume was sent to press, viz., the Appendix having this title in *The Messages of Jesus according to the Synoptists*, by Thomas C. Hall, D.D., Scribner's Sons, 1901.

¹⁸ And again, Whoso sweareth by the
   altar, it is nothing ;
   but whoso sweareth by the gift that
   is on the altar is bound by his oath.
¹⁹ Ye blind ; for which is greater, the
   gift, or the altar that makes the
   gift holy ? *

²⁰ He, then, who sweareth by the altar
   sweareth by it, and by all the things
   on it,
²¹ And he who sweareth by the sanctuary
   sweareth by it, and by Him who in-
   habiteth it,
²² And he that sweareth by heaven
   sweareth by the throne of God, and
   by Him that sitteth upon it.
²⁴ Ye blind guides, which filter out a
   gnat, and swallow a camel ! †

---

* For the literary structure compare the twofold illustrations of scribal righteousness in the Sermon on the
Mount, Mt. 5 : 21-22, 27-28, 31-32. Also with the general statement verse 15, followed by 16, 18, and 20-22,
each ending with the refrain 17, 19, 24, compare Mt.
6 : 1, 2-4, 5-6, 16-18.

† That portion of Mt. 23 which is found nowhere else
seems to form a discourse against the scribes for their
false casuistry. Of 16-22 we have spoken. Verses 15
and 24 seem to be connected. "Blind guides" re-
calls Mt. 15 : 14.

Jesus reiterates in Private to the Twelve his Repudiation of the Scribes and their Traditions

The ' Hedge of the Law ' shall be rooted up

Mt. 15 : 12–13

Mt. 15 [12] Then the disciples came near and say unto him, Knowest thou that the Pharisees when they heard that saying * were scandalized? [13] But he answered and said : —

> Every plant which my heavenly Father hath not planted shall be rooted up.

Blindness of Soul Fatal and Incurable

Mt. 15 : 14 ; 6 : 22–23 = Lk. 6 : 39 ; 11 : 34–35[36] = Jn. 9 : 39–41 ; 10 : 1–6

" 23 : 24.

> Mt. 15 [14] Let them alone ; **they are blind leaders of the blind** *"*; **but if the blind lead the blind, both shall fall into the ditch.**

* The reference in the context is to the revolutionary utterance by which Jesus, as our second evangelist remarks, had swept away the Mosaic distinctions of clean and unclean meats. The disciples now somewhat timidly inquire if Jesus realizes the effect of his utterances on the religious authorities. The occasion is by Matthew made the same as that when the disciples (Mt., " Peter ") ask an explanation of the saying, and this is doubtless correct but as the Markan form is clearly the more original, we have permitted the digression to stand in the unchronological Markan order (see above, p. 221).

6 [22] The lamp of the body is the eye ; if thine
eye be pure thy whole body shall be lit up.
[23] But if thine eye be false,[a] thy whole body
shall be dark.   If, therefore, the very light
that is in thee be darkness, how great is
the darkness.*

[a] Mk. 7 : 22;
3 : 22.

V. Third Discourse of the Crisis in Galilee. The Scribes and Pharisees demand a Sign from Heaven

Occasion

After coming out from the scene of controversy in the Pharisee's house, the scribes and
Pharisees meet Jesus with violent opposition.

Lk. 11 : 53–12 : 1 (*auplicate* 11 : 29ª)

Lk. 11 [53] And when he came out thence
the scribes and Pharisees began to press him
violently, and to cross-examine him on many
points, lying in wait for him to seize some word
from his lips.

* This passage from the Matthæan Sermon on the
Mount appears from the setting of the parallels in Luke
and John to have been uttered on occasion of the blasphemous insinuation of the Jerusalem scribes.   V. 23
thus appears in the light of an explanation of the awful
utterance about the sin that hath never forgiveness, and is
a further link to connect it with the denunciation of the
blind leaders of the blind, and the warning against an
" evil eye."   See Appendix A (8), p. 150.

They demand a Sign from Heaven

Mt. 12 : 38 (*duplicate* 16 : 1) = Mk. 8 : 11 = Lk. 11 : 16
= Jn. 6 : 30-31

Mt. 12 ³⁸ Then certain of the scribes and Pharisees answered him saying, Teacher, we would see a sign from thee.

Jesus' Reply: The Sign of Jonah

Mt. 12: 39-42 (*duplicate* 16: 2-4) = Mk. 8 : 12 = Lk. 11: 29-31

Mt. 12 ³⁹ But he answered and said unto them : —

> A wicked and adulterous generation
> seeketh after a sign
> and no sign shall be given it
> save the sign of Jonah the prophet.

| ⁴⁰ For like as Jonah was in the seamonster's belly three days and three nights so shall the Son of Man be in the heart of the earth three days and three nights. | Lk. 11 ³⁰ For just as Jonah was himself a sign to the men of Nineveh, so shall the Son of Man be to this generation.* |

* The parallel explanations of "the sign of Jonah" above given are both absent from the alternate version, Mk. 8: 11-12 = Mt. 16: 1-4. That of Luke 11: 30 has at least the merit of being conceivably correct, since it agrees with the facts of the O. T. narrative, wherein

⁴¹ The men of Nineveh shall arise in the judgment
  together with this generation
  and shall condemn it ;
  for they repented at the preaching of Jonah,
  and lo, a greater matter than Jonah is here.

Jonah's preaching to the Ninevites is peculiarly characterized by the very fact that they neither ask nor receive
miraculous authentication of his exhortation and warning, and further agrees with its own context (v. 32) in
which Jesus points out this contrast with the generation
that demands a sign. That of Mt. 12 : 40 is absolutely
excluded by its contradiction of the context, missing the
real point of comparison, and substituting the trivial and
inapposite one of the three (?) days of Jesus' lying in
the grave. But in my judgment the most genuine form
of the tradition is that which excludes both, both being
attempts of later reporters to explain this enigmatic saying of Jesus. In point of fact Jesus did believe that one
great sign had been given, but had remained unobserved
because the adulterous generation was blind to divine
portents in its craze for superstition (Lk. 17 : 20–21).
Elias, whose coming to prepare Israel by repentance for
the great " day of Jehovah " was God's appointed sign of
the Son of Man, had come, " and they did unto him as
they listed." It was shortly after this that the disciples
learned from Jesus' lips how deep a significance he attached to the appearance and fate of John the Baptist
(Mk. 9 : 13). Now the succeeding context, Mt. 12 : 41–
42, accuses this wicked generation of a twofold obduracy
put to shame by the very heathen of the O. T. They

> [42] The Queen of the South shall arise in the
> judgment
> together with this generation
> and shall condemn it ;
> for she came from the ends of the earth

have rejected a great proclamation of repentance like that of Jonah though the men of Nineveh did not, and they have also rejected the winning entreaty of the divine wisdom (see above, p. 225, note on the Jewish conception of 'wisdom' as the redemptive agency of God's fatherly love), though the Queen of Sheba did not. It is possible that in both cases Jesus was referring to his own preaching ; but (1) the enigmatic reference to the former as a "sign," (2) the analogy of other passages in which Jesus couples together their treatment of John the Baptist and himself (Mt. 11 : 16–19, 17 : 10–13 ; Lk. 7 : 29–30) and declares John greater than all earlier prophets (Lk. 7 : 24–28), and (3) the contrast so bold a reference to himself as greater than Jonah and Solomon would present to Jesus' invariable reserve regarding his own personality in public address, suggest rather that only the latter of the two comparisons refers to his own preaching, the former referring to the Baptist's message of repentance so like that of Jonah. This view is further corroborated by the admirable appropriateness which then appears in the succeeding context of Matthew, the Parable of the House Swept and Garnished, whose application is expressly declared to be to " this evil generation." It had seemed to purge itself at the preaching of the Baptist, but did not admit God's Spirit, the rightful tenant, when He came to His abode.

to hear the wisdom of Solomon
and lo, a greater matter than Solomon is
here.*

Parable of the House Swept and Garnished

Mt. 12 : 43–45 = Lk. 11 : 24–26

Mt. 12 43 Whenever an unclean spirit goes out
from a man, it passes through arid places seeking for rest and findeth none. 44 Then it saith, I
will return unto my abode whence I came
forth ; and it cometh and findeth it empty and
swept and garnished. 45 Then it goeth and
taketh to itself seven other spirits worse than
itself, and they come in and take up their abode
there, and the last state of that man becomes
worse than the first. So shall it be also unto
this wicked generation.†

* *I.e.* the gracious call of God extended through Jesus
to repentant sinners.

† Matthew is clearly correct in regarding this parable
as applying to the wicked generation purged by the baptism of John but untenanted by the Spirit sent with the
Messiah, and not, with Luke, as a mere comparison of
the permanence of Jesus' exorcisms with those of the
Pharisees. But this being so it can hardly be otherwise
than part of the extended discourse which Matthew gives
as preceding.

Spiritual Kindred; an Episode and Saying

Mk. 3: 20-21, 31-32 = Mt. 12: 46-50 = Lk. 8: 19-21
(*duplicate*, 11: 27-28)

Mk. 3 ²⁰[And he cometh home; and the crowd cometh together again so that they could not even eat bread. ²¹ And when his kindred heard it they went forth to lay hands on him, for they said to themselves, He is beside himself * * *].* And there come his mother and his brethren, and standing outside they sent a message to him calling him forth. ³² And a crowd was sitting around him, and they tell him, Lo, thy mother and thy brethren are outside asking for thee. Lk. 11 ²⁷[And it came to pass as he

---

* This description probably refers to the same scene as described above (p. 231) in the language of Lk. 11 : 53-12 : 1. Mark appends the story to his account of the choosing of the Twelve for the sake of the saying, " My mother and brethren are they that hear," etc. Matthew and Luke omit this introduction. Between 21 and 31 Mark again inserts the blasphemy of the scribes, thus making it a foil for the venial sin of Jesus' mother and brethren, who said only ἔξεστιν. But the *logian* version of the saying in Lk. 11 : 27, widely as it varies from the Markan, which Luke repeats in 8 : 19-21, is close enough to prove identity, and this also is connected (perhaps improperly) with the same occasion. Mark's displacement, accordingly, is but slight.

was saying these things]* a certain woman out
of the crowd lifted up her voice and said to him,
Blessed is the womb that bare thee and the
breasts which thou didst suck. ²⁸But he said,
Nay, rather blessed are they that hear the word
of God and keep it.

Mk. 3 ³⁴ And looking round on those who
were sitting in a circle about him he saith, Behold my mother and my brethren.

VI. Fourth Discourse of the Galilean Crisis. Jesus warns against the Leaven (Bread) of the Pharisees

Mk. 8: 13–21 = Mt. 16: 5–12 = Lk. 12: 1 = Jn. 6: 30–35

Occasion

Mk. 8 ¹³ And he left them † and entering again
into the boat he departed to the other side.

---

* The reference is to the parable of the House Swept
and Garnished, but the woman's ejaculation is occasioned
— if we may judge by what Mark relates of the occasion
of the *logion* — by the message that Jesus' mother was
outside.

† The reference is to the Pharisees who had demanded
the Sign from Heaven, this one of Mark's sources having nothing more to tell of the crisis than the simple
fact of the demand and Jesus' refusal, Mk. 8: 10–13.

[14] And they had forgotten to take bread, and had no more than a single loaf with them in the boat. [15] And he was charging them, saying, "Take heed, beware of the leaven of the Pharisees, and of the leaven of Herod." * [16] And they were debating with one another, "It is because we have no bread." [17] And when he perceived it he saith unto them : —

> Why are ye in debate because ye have no bread?
>
> Do ye not yet perceive nor understand?
>
> Have ye your heart made callous?
>
> [18] Having eyes see ye not,
>
> and having ears hear ye not?
>
> And do ye not remember
>
> [19] when I brake the five loaves among the five thousand

* The warning against the teaching of the Pharisees under the simile of bread (Mt. 16: 12), following as it does upon the Feeding of the Multitude, Messianic Murmurs, and Demand of a Sign from Heaven, has its counterpart in the Discourse on the True Bread from Heaven in John. Luke also (12: 1) has the bare statement that this parabolic warning was given at this time. But the Synoptic narrative, while suggesting the possibility of some extended discourse on this subject, concerns itself only with the concluding words of Jesus when in the boat he rebuked his disciples for their lack of insight and lack of faith.

how many hampers full of broken pieces ye
took up?

²⁰ They say unto him, Twelve.

And when the seven among the four thousand

how many baskets full of broken pieces took
ye up?*

²¹ And they say unto him, Seven.

And he said unto them

Do ye not yet understand?

²²ᵃ And they come unto Bethsaida.

VII. Warnings of Impending Judgment

Sayings principally reported in Lk. 12: 35–13: 35

(1) *On the Futility of Dependence on Privilege*

Occasion

Lk. 13: 22–23

Lk. 13 ²² And he was passing through cities
and villages, teaching and journeying on toward
Jerusalem. ²³ And a certain man said to him,
Lord, are those that are saved few in number?

---

* The compiler of our second gospel here combines
the two versions of the Feeding of the Multitude. From
the connection it would appear to be the version of
8: 1–10 (*Four* thousand) with which the passage was
originally connected.

Parable of the Narrow Door

Lk. 13: 24 = Mt. 7: 13–14

And he said unto them : —

> [24] Strive hard to enter by the narrow door,
>
> for many, I tell you, will seek to enter in
>
> and will not be able.

Mt. 7 [13] For wide is the gate and spacious the way

> that leadeth to destruction
>
> and many are they that pass in by it.

[14] For narrow is the gate and strait-ened[a] the way

> that leadeth unto life
>
> and few are they that find it.

_a Acts 14: 22.

Many who claim a Place in the Kingdom will be Rejected

Mt. 7: 21–23 = Lk. 13: 26–27 *

Mt. 7 [21] Not everyone that saith unto me Lord, Lord,

> shall enter into the kingdom of God,

* While it is quite clear that this logion is out of place in the Sermon on the Mount (see Appendix A (11), p. 166),

> but he that doeth the will of my
> Father which is in heaven.
> [22] Many will say (to the king) in that
> day,

Lk. 13 [26] We did eat and drink in thy presence
    and thou didst teach * (?) in our
    streets ;

especially in the Matthæan form, which makes it apply
to false teachers in the church (7 : 22, contrast Lk.
13 : 26), it is much less easy to assign it its true position.
True the occasion is well defined in Lk. 13 : 22–24, but
warnings of judgment to come must have been a constant feature in the preaching of Jesus (Mk. 1 : 15), and
there are utterances with which the present might seem
to have a closer relation than with the Lucan context ;
for example, the Dirge upon the Galilean Cities reported
by both Luke (10 : 13–16) and Matthew (11 : 20–24) in
connection with the Mission of the Disciples in Galilee
(cf. Lk. 13 : 26 with 10 : 13). The combined authority
of Matthew and Luke forbids our transferring hither the
Dirge, appropriately as it might lead in the question, Lk.
13 : 23, and subsequent discourse We prefer to remain
in doubt as to an original relation between the elements
of Lk. 13 : 22–30. In particular Lk. 13 : 30 has better
connection in Mt. 19 : 30 ; 20 : 16, and the parable of the
Closed Door (v. 25 = Mt. 25 : 1–13) is quite artificially
brought in. But Matthew should not have removed
verses 28–29 to place them after the story of the Believing Centurion (8 : 1–10).

 * The word "teach" reflects upon Jesus' own career.
"Walk" is more likely to have been the original.

R

and he * will say,
I tell you I never knew you ;
begone from me all ye workers of
wickedness.[a]

[a] Mt. 25 : 41.

Abrahamic Descent a Worthless Dependence

Mt. 8 : 11–12 = Lk. 13 : 28–29

Mt. 8 [11] And I tell you that many shall come
from east and west and shall take their
places at the feast with Abraham, Isaac
and Jacob in the kingdom of God.   [12] But
the sons of the kingdom shall go forth into
the outer darkness ; there shall be weeping
and gnashing of teeth.[b]

[b] Mt. 24 : 51 ;
25 : 30.

* The Lucan form, which puts this judgment in the
mouth of the Messianic Judge spoken of in the third
person, is alone conceivable at any time previous to
Jesus' full revelation of his Messianic character.   Even
then the " I " could only have been spoken in the inner
circle of the Twelve.   It is indeed probable that these
parables of the judgment belong to the period subsequent to Cæsarea Philippi, but even so the " I will say "
seems less probable in the mouth of Jesus.   Besides this
the Matthæan form clearly shows adaptation to the conditions of a church already troubled by false teachers.
We ventured also the opinion that the original utterance
will have had " walk " rather than " teach," the reference
of which to Jesus himself would have been so obvious.

(2) *Real Basis of the Messianic Judgment*

Parable of the Shepherd dividing his Flock

Mt. 25: 31-46

Mt. 25 [31] But when the Son of Man shall come
in his glory and all the angels with
him,

then shall he sit upon his 'throne of
glory,'

[32] and all the nations shall be gathered
together before him,

and he shall separate them one man
from another,

as a shepherd separates sheep from
goats.

[33] And he shall set the sheep on his
right hand, and the goats on his
left.

[34] Then shall the king say to those on
his right hand,

Come ye that were blessed of my
Father,

inherit the kingdom that was prepared for you from the foundation
of the world.

[35] For I was hungry and ye gave me to
eat,

thirsty and ye gave me to drink,

a stranger and ye took me in,

naked and ye clothed me,
I was sick and ye visited me,
in prison and ye came to me.

[37] Then will the righteous answer him and say,
Sir, when did we see thee hungry and feed thee,
or thirsty and give thee drink?
[38] And when did we see thee a stranger and took thee in,
or naked and clothed thee?
[39] When did we see thee sick or in prison and came to thee?

[40] And the king will answer and say to them,
I tell you of a truth,
By so much as ye did it to one of these brethren of mine,
these men of very small account,
ye did it to me.[a]

[a] Mk. 9: 37, 41;
Prov. 19: 17.

[41] Then will he speak to those on his left,
Begone from me, ye accurst,
into the everlasting fire prepared for the Devil and his angels.
[42] For I was hungry and ye gave me naught to eat,
thirsty and ye gave me no drink,
[43] a stranger and ye took me not in,
naked and ye clothed me not,
sick and in prison and ye visited me not.

⁴⁴ Then these too will answer and say,
Sir, when did we see thee hungry or thirsty,
or a stranger, or naked,
or sick, or in prison,
and did thee no service?

⁴⁵ Then he will answer them, saying,
I tell you of a truth,
By so much as ye did it not to one of these
men of very small account,
ye also did it not to me.

⁴⁶ And these shall go away into everlasting
punishment,
but the righteous into everlasting life.

A Connected Incident

Lk. 13 : 31–33

Lk. 13 ³¹ At that same hour there came up
certain Pharisees and said to him, Depart, and
get away hence, for Herod desireth to kill thee.
³² And he said to them, Go, and tell that jackal:
Lo, I cast out demons and perform my healings
to-day and to-morrow, and on the third day I
shall be through. ³³ But I must needs go on to-
day and to-morrow and the next day, for it cannot be that a prophet should perish except in
Jerusalem.

(3) *Be Ready to give Account in the Judgment*

Occasion

Lk. 17 : 20ᵃ

Lk. 17 ²⁰ᵃ And being asked by the Pharisees when the kingdom of God cometh, he answered them and said : —

No Prognostication will avail to date the Parousia

Lk. 17 : 20ᵇ-21 (= Mk. 13 : 21 = Mt. 24 : 23?)

Lk. 17 ²⁰ᵇ The kingdom of God cometh not with taking of observations, neither shall people say, Lo, here, or there. ²¹ For behold, the kingdom of God is among you.

The Signs of the Times are Enough to prove it Near

Lk. 12 : 54-56 = Mt. 16 : 2-3 (β text)

Lk. 12 ⁵⁴ Whenever ye see a cloud rising in the west,

at once ye say, There is rain coming ;
and so it comes to pass.

⁵⁵ And whenever the south wind blows,
ye say, There will be scorching heat ;
and so it comes to pass.

⁵⁶ Ye hypocrites,

ye know how to take account of the
appearance of earth and heaven ;
how is it that ye know not how to
take account of this epoch ?

*Be reconciled ere too Late with him who is
bringing his Suit against Israel*

Lk. 12 : 57–59 = Mt. 5 : 25–26

Lk. 12 ⁵⁷ And why even of your own selves do
ye not judge what is right ? ⁵⁸ For as thou
art going with him who is suing thee before
the magistrate, do thy utmost to effect a
settlement with him on the road, lest perhaps he drag thee before the judge, and the
judge deliver thee to the sheriff and the
sheriff cast thee into prison. ⁵⁹ I tell thee,
Thou shalt never come out thence till thou
have paid the last farthing.

A Warning based on Current Events

Lk. 13 : 1–5

Jesus told of the Fate of Pilate's Victims

Occasion

Lk. 13 ¹ And there were some present on that
same occasion who informed him concerning the
Galileans whose blood Pilate had mingled with

that of their sacrifices.   ²And he answered and
said unto them : —

> Suppose ye that these Galileans were sinful
> beyond all the men of Galilee
> because they suffered these things?
> ³ I tell you, Nay,
> but except ye repent
> ye shall all perish in a like manner.

> ⁴ Or those eighteen
> on whom the tower fell in Siloam and killed
> them,
> suppose ye that they were transgressors
> beyond all the men that dwell in Jerusalem?
> ⁵ I tell you, Nay,
> but except ye repent
> ye shall all perish in a like manner.

Parable of the Barren Fig Tree

Lk. 13 : 6–9

Lk. 13 ⁶ And he spake this parable : —

A certain man had a fig tree planted in his
vineyard, and he came seeking fruit on it,
and found none.   ⁷ And he said to the vine
dresser, See here, it is now three years that
I have come to seek fruit on this fig tree,
and I find none ; cut it down ; why should
it make the ground useless as well?   ⁸ But

he answered and said to him, Master, leave it alone for this one year more, till I have digged and put dung about it, ⁹and if it bear fruit thereafter, very well; but if not, cut it down.*

---

* The *parable* of the barren fig tree should not be identified with the *incident* (Mk. 11:12–14, 20–25 = Mt. 21:18–22), though Luke's omission of the latter is doubtless for this reason, just as he omits Mk. 14:3–9 in view of Lk. 7:36–50. The *incident*, which properly ends with Mk. 11:14 (compare Mt. 21:19) is too clearly dated, and that in spite of the evangelist's consciousness of the discrepancy in the season of year (Mk. 11:13ᵇ), to allow it to be set aside. We may understand the occurrence as simply an application by Jesus of the methods of prophetic symbolism (cf. Ez. 39:17). The precocious promise of a fig tree thus early (March — April) in full leaf, attracting his attention as he goes from Bethany toward Jerusalem, he approaches, only to find it as barren of the budding fruit as its flourishing appearance gave reason to expect the contrary. The curse thereupon pronounced has no reference to the tree, save as a type and symbol of the outwardly promising, inwardly barren Israel. Hence in its first form the story must have ended with the utterance, "No man eat fruit of thee henceforth forever." The rest is the work of our evangelists, Matthew and Mark, who, each in his own way, seek to piece out what they regard as an incomplete account. Both assume a visible effect upon the tree, Matthew instantly (παραχρῆμα, a Lucan word, not found elsewhere in Matthew), Mark the next day;

(4) *Suddenness of the Parousia*

The Day of the Lord will come like the Flood

Mt. 24 : 37–39 = Lk. 17 : 26–27

Mt. 24 [37] And as were the days of Noah
so shall be the Coming of the Son
of Man.

[38] For as people were in the days before the cataclysm
eating and drinking, marrying and
giving in marriage
until the day that Noah entered into
the ark,

[39] and knew not until the flood came
and swept them all away ;
so shall be also the Coming of the
Son of Man.

and Mark further attaches two *logia*, one (Mk. 11 : 22–
24) rightly located by Matthew in 17 : 20, the other
(11 : 25) located by Matthew no better than here in
6 : 14–15. Mk. 11 : 20–21 is editorial solder. If the
reader be indisposed to grant the possibility of both a
parable and, subsequently, an incident of a barren fig
tree, then it is far better to suppose that the parable has
been elaborated from the symbolic utterance, as some
derive Lk. 15 : 11–32 from Mt. 21 : 28–31, or Mt. 25 : 1–
13 from Lk. 13 : 25, than *vice versa*. Mk. 11 : 12–14
must be accepted as historical.

Or like the Judgment upon Sodom

Lk. 17 : 28–30

Lk. 17 ²⁸ Just as it happened likewise in the days of Lot.

    They were eating, drinking, buying, selling, planting, building.

    ²⁹ But in the day that Lot went forth out of Sodom

      it rained fire and brimstone from heaven and destroyed them all.

    ³⁰ After the same manner shall it be in the day when the Son of Man is revealed.

One shall be taken, Another left

Mt. 24 : 40–41 = Lk. 17 : 34–35

Mt. 24 ⁴⁰ Then shall there be two men in the field ;

    one shall be taken and the other left.

    ⁴¹ There shall be two women grinding at the mill ;

    one shall be taken and the other left.

Carrion calls its own Scavengers

Lk. 17 : 37 = Mt. 24 : 28

Lk. 17 ³⁷ And they answered him and say, Where, Lord? But he said unto them : —

> Wherever the carcase is
> there the vultures will be gathered
> together.

A Warning against False Alarms of the Parousia

Lk. 17 : 22

Lk. 17 [22] And he said unto the disciples : —
> Days will come when ye will long to
> see one of the days of the Son of
> Man
> and ye shall not see it.

The Reality will admit no Mistake

Mt. 24 : 26–27 = Lk. 17 : 23–24

Mt. 24 [26] If, therefore, they say to you, Lo, he
> is in the wilderness,
> go not forth ;
> Lo, he is in his chambers,
> believe it not.
> [27] For even as the lightning cometh
> forth from the east and shineth
> unto the west ;
> so shall be the Parousia of the Son
> of Man.

Lk. 17 [25] But first must he suffer many things and be
rejected of this generation.

(5) *Parables on being Ready for the Parousia*

The Ten Virgins

Mt. 25 : 1–12 = Lk. 12 : 35–38; 13 : 25 *

Mt. 25 ¹ Then shall the kingdom of God be likened to ten virgins which took their lamps and went forth to meet the bridegroom and the bride.† ² And five of them were foolish, and five prudent. ³ For the foolish took their lamps, but took no oil

---

* We have seen above (p. 166), in connection with Mt. 7 : 21–23 = Lk. 13 : 23–27, that Lk. 13 : 25 is an embellishment not originally part of the saying about the narrow door. The figure of fruitless attempts to enter the "door" of the kingdom leads to its introduction. We have here a parallel to Luke's treatment of Mk. 14 : 3–9 which he omits, though borrowing a trait or two to embellish his own story of the Penitent Harlot (7 : 36–50; cf. verses 37ᵇ, 38ᵇ, 46, with Mark). It does not necessarily follow that Mt. 25 : 1–12 was known to Luke otherwise than by oral tradition. In fact, the omission of a narrative so largely dependent for intelligibility on knowledge of Oriental customs would not be strange in a gospel which omits Mk. 7 : 1–24. But in reality Lk. 12 : 35–38 is a strict parallel, though in this version of the parable the peculiarly Oriental features are subordinated.

† "And the bride" is an addition of the Western text, which is at least necessary to the sense.

with them ; ⁴ but the prudent took oil in
their vessels with their lamps. ⁵ And while
the bridegroom delayed they all slumbered
and slept. ⁶ But at midnight there arose a
cry : Lo, the bridegroom ; come forth to
meet him. ⁷ Then all those virgins rose up
and trimmed their lamps. ⁸ And the foolish said to the prudent, Give us of your oil,
for our lamps are going out. ⁹ But the prudent answered and said, Nay, lest there be
not enough for us and you ; go rather to
the dealers and buy for yourselves. ¹⁰ And
while they were gone to buy, the bridegroom came ; and they that were ready
went in with him to the wedding,* and the
door was shut. ¹¹ Later came the other
virgins also and said, Sir, Sir, open unto us.
¹² But he answered and said, Of a truth I
know you not.

*To the Prince of this World the Son of Man
comes as a Thief: to Believers as a Master
to Waiting Servants*

Lk. 12: 39–46 = Mt. 24: 42–51 = Mk. 13: 33–37

Lk. 12 ³⁹ This ye know, that if the householder
had known at what hour the thief was com-

---

* The additional traits of Lk. 12: 37–38 seem to be derived from verses 43–44 and Lk. 22: 26–27; cf. Mt. 24: 47.

ing, he would not have allowed his house
to be broken into.[a] [40] You too should be
prepared, because the Son of Man will
come in an hour when you are not expect-
ing it.

a Mk. 3 : 27;
1 Thess. 5 : 2.

[41] Peter said unto him, Sir, are you speaking
this parable to us, or even to all? [42] And the
Lord said : —

Who, then, is the faithful and prudent
steward, whom the master will set over his
household to distribute provisions as required? [43] That slave is to be congratulated whom his master finds so doing when
he comes. [44] I tell you of a truth he will
set him over all his property. [45] But if that
slave says to himself, My master is defer-
ring his coming, and begins to beat the
servants and maids, and to eat and drink
and be drunken, [46] the master of that slave
will come in a day that he expects him not,
and an hour of which he knows not, and
will cut him in pieces, and appoint him his
lot with the unfaithful.[b]

b Mt. 21 : 41
and ‖ ‖.

The foregoing seven discourses, which manifest a greater or less degree of internal connection, must suffice to illustrate the possibilities of
synthetic reconstruction of the greater discourses

of the Lord. We have not included the Jerusalem discourses, though that on the Doom of
Jerusalem and the Certainty of the Speedy
Coming of the Son of Man, Mt. 24 = Mk. 13 =
Lk. 21, commonly called The Eschatological
Discourse, is at first sight well adapted to bear
out the contention that more than mere apophthegms and sayings have survived to us. Moreover the section Mk. 13 : 28–32 = Mt. 24 : 32–
36 (*duplicate* Mt. 5 : 18 = Lk. 16 : 17) = Lk.
21 (22 ?) : 29–33 ; Acts 1 : 7 would seem to be
the original source of the saying Mt. 5 : 18, now
embedded in the Sermon on the Mount. With
much more confidence we can assign the teaching on How to Discriminate between True and
False Teachers, also now incorporated in the
Sermon on the Mount (Mt. 7 : 15–16 [20?] =
Lk. 6 : 44), to the discourse of Warning against
the Spirit of the Scribes, Mk. 12 : 38–40 = Mt.
23 : 1–10 = Lk. 20 : 45–47.* Mark here has set
an unfortunate example of combination by attaching verses 38ᵇ–39 from the Denunciation of
the Scribes (see above, p. 222), and Matthew
goes still further by adding verses 4 (= Lk.

* See Appendix A (10), p. 161.

11 : 46), 6–7^a (= Lk. 11 : 43; Markan form, Mk. 13 : 38^b–39 = Lk. 20 : 46), 11 (Markan form, Mk. 10 : 43 = Mt. 20 : 26–27 = Lk. 22 : 26–27), and 12 (= Lk. 14 : 11 = 18 : 14). In reality the Denunciation *uttered to* the Pharisees and Scribes, in Galilee, and the Warning of the Twelve against the *Spirit of* the Scribes, in Jerusalem, should be distinguished, as the Lucan narrative makes clear; and it is with the latter that we would connect Mt. 7 : 15–16 = Lk. 6 : 44. If we may judge by the obvious interrelation of the Farewell Discourse, Jn. 15–16, with the *second* Mission of the Twelve, Lk. 22 : 35–38, and with Mt. 10 : 16–33, this is also the true place for the two sayings now incorporated in the Sermon on the Mount, Lk. 6 : 40 = Mt. 10 : 24–25 = Jn. 15 : 20 (13 : 16), and parts of Mt. 5 : 14–16 (cf. Jn. 8 : 12, Mk. 4 : 21, and Oxyrhyn. *Logia*, No. vii). Similarly there is much to indicate that the teaching on Reconciliation as better than Sacrifice, Mt. 5 : 23, and the Command to Forgive, Mt. 6 : 14–15, once belonged in the context of Mt. 18 : 6–7, 10, 15–17, 21–35, and the Call to Unsparing Renunciation, Mt. 5 : 29–30 = Mk. 9 : 43–48 = Mt. 18 : 8–9,

s

and Parable of the Savourless Salt, Mt. 5 : 13 =
Lk. 14 : 34–35 = Mk. 9 : 50ᵃ, belong in that of
Lk. 14 : 28–35.*

But it is not our purpose to discover a setting
for every fragment included in the Sermon on
the Mount ; nor shall we include discourses of
the Galilean period which show no signs of connection with these fragments, though such as the
Eulogy of the Baptist and Dirge over the Cities
of Galilee, Mt. 11 : 1–24 = Lk. 7 : 18–35 ; 10 : 13–
17, or the Parabolic Discourse on the lake-shore,
Mt. 13 : 1–52 = Mk. 4 : 1–34 = Lk. 8 : 1–18, are
surely more than mere aggregations of scattered
utterances by evangelic compilers. The seven
discourses above given will suffice to illustrate
what may be done when the attempts at synthesis of these early compilers are removed. Doubtless there will be comparatively little which will
fully vindicate itself to the judgment of our readers as a whole ; but a little in this direction will
amply justify the task. May the bringing together of seemingly kindred utterances of the
Lord give new light on the meaning of the sev-
ered parts.

* See Appendix A (6), p. 145.

INDEX TO SCRIPTURE PASSAGES
DISCUSSED

		Page Number				Page Number
Ps.	37 : 11	116, 127, 175	Mt.	5 : 29–30	.	80, 257
	91 : 4	. . 225		5 : 31–32	. .	89
	123 : 2	. . 150		5 : 32 .	.	117, 177
Eccl.	1 : 12, 16; 2 : 1–17	70		5 : 33–37	. .	90
Jere.	31 : 35–37 .	. 136		5 : 37 .	. .	179
Amos	3 : 10	. . 219		5 : 38–42	. .	91
Mt.	3 : 15	. . 135		5 : 39 .	. .	179
	4 : 4	. . 42		5 : 43–48	. .	92
	4 : 24–25 .	65–68, 83, 121, 124		6 : 1–6 .	. .	95–97
				6 : 1–18 .	.	39, 146
	5 : 1–12 .	85, 125		6 : 7–15	72–73, 146, 181– 186	
	5 : 4–5 .	. 175				
	5 : 5	. . 127		6 : 14–15	. .	148, 257
	5 : 13	. . 258		6 : 16–18	. .	98
	5 : 13–16 .	. 130		6 : 18 .	.	180
	5 : 17, 19–20	87, 133, 138		6 : 19–20	. .	154
				6 : 19–34	69–72, 148–156, 186–191	
	5 : 14–16 .	. 257				
	5 : 18–19 .	6, 133–138, 256		6 : 22–23	149, 155, 231	
				6 : 24 .	.	153, 196
	5 : 21–22 .	. 88		7 : 1–5 .	. .	99
	5 : 21–26 .	. 138		7 : 1–27 .	. .	156
	5 : 22–23 .	. 177		7 : 3–5 .	. .	158
	5 : 23	. . 257		7 : 6 .	.	159, 203
	5 : 23–26 .	80, 138		7 : 7–11 .	.	160, 185
	5 : 27–28 .	. 89		7 : 12 .	.	91, 160
	5 : 27–32 .	. 140		7 : 13–14	. .	240

			Page Number					Page Number
Mt.	7 : 13–20	.	161	Mt.	19 : 16–22	.	.	11
	7 : 15–16	.	257		20 : 1–16	.	.	15
	7 : 17	.	165		21 : 18–22	.	.	249
	7 : 18	.	100		23 : 12	.	.	201
	7 : 19–20	.	166		23 : 15–22, 24 .		227–229
	7 : 21–27	100, 166, 180		23 : 16–22	.	91, 227
	7 : 28–29	.	102, 167		23 : 27	.	.	222
	8 : 1–13	.	167		23 : 34–39	.	.	225
	8 : 2–4	.	134		24 : 26–27	.	.	252
	8 : 5–10, 13	.	102, 170		24 : 37–39	.	.	250
	8 : 11–12	.	242		24 : 37–25 : 46	.	171
	9 : 32–34	.	151		24 : 40–41	.	.	251
	10 : 16–33	.	257		25 : 1–12	.	.	253
	10 : 24–25	.	257		25 : 14–30	.	193–195
	11 : 1–13, 14–15	.	147		25 : 31–46	.	243–245
	12 : 15–16	. 83, 121, 124	Mk.	1 : 7–8	.	.	19
	12 : 22–45	.	151		1 : 15	.	.	212
	12 : 22–50	.	203		1 : 21–28	.	.	172
	12 : 23–24	.	210		1 : 22	.	.	102
	12 : 25–32	.	212–215		1 : 24	.	.	212
	12 : 33, 35	.	100, 215		2 : 1–3 : 6	.	.	121
	12 : 34, 36–37 .	.	215		3 : 7–14	65–68, 83–84,
	12 : 34	.	165				121, 123
	12 : 38–42	.	232–235		3 : 7–6 : 12	.	.	122
	12 : 43–45	.	235		3 : 11–12	.	.	212
	12 : 46–50	.	236		3 : 13–35	.	.	122
	14 : 25–35	.	145		3 : 19–35	.	.	122
	15 : 12–13	.	230		3 : 20–21, 31–32	.	236
	15 : 14	.	230		3 : 22–30	122, 151, 212–
	16 : 1–12	.	151				213
	17 : 1–4	.	143		4 : 1–34	.	.	122
	18 : 1–8	.	146		4 : 10–25	.	.	132
	18 : 6–7, 10, 15–17,				4 : 11–12	.	.	132
	21–35	.	257		4 : 21–22	.	130, 132
	18 : 6, 8–9	.	140		4 : 35–5 : 43	.	.	122
	18 : 21–35	.	148		6 : 1–6	.	.	122
	19 : 9	.	117		6 : 3	.	.	101

		Page Number				Page Number
Mk.	6:30–7:31; 8:34–35; 9:2-10 .	217	Lk.	6:40 . . .	257
	7:1-23 .	151, 217		6:41-42 . .	158
	7:6-13 . .	219		6:43-45	100, 161-165
	7:14-23 . .	220		6:44 . . .	257
	7:32-37; 8:1-22, 27-38; 9:1–11:13 .	217		6:46-49	100, 166, 180
	8:1-10 . .	205		7:1 . .	102, 167
	8:11-21 . .	151		7:1-10	102, 167, 170
	8:13-21 .	237-239		7:36-50 . .	253
	8:22-26	206-208, 217		8:16 . .	130, 132
	9:33-50 . .	143		11:1-4 . . .	73
	9:42-49 .	140, 142		11:1-13 .	181-186
	10:10-11 . .	140		11:14-12:1 . .	203
	10:17-31 . .	11		11:17-23; 12:10	212-215
	11:12-14, 20-25	148, 249		11:24-26 . .	235
	12:38-40 .	222, 256		11:27-28 . .	236
	13:28-32 . .	256		11:29-31 . .	232
	14:3-9 . . .	253		11:29-32, 34-36	150-153
Lk.	4:16-30 . . .	20		11:33-36	130, 132, 148
	5:12-16 . .	167		11:37-38 . .	216
	6:12-19 . .	65		11:39-41 . .	218
	6:17-19 .	121, 124		11:42-44 . .	222
	6:20-23 .	85, 125		11:45-47 . .	223
	6:21, 22, 23, 25, 26 .	175-176		11:48-51 . .	224
	6:24-26 .	39, 86, 125		11:53-12:1 . .	231
	6:27 . . .	38		12:1, 10 . .	151
	6:27-28 . .	92		12:13-34 .	69-72, 155, 186-190
	6:27-38 . .	78		12:35-38 . .	253
	6:29-31 . .	91		12:39-46 .	254-255
	6:32-36 . .	92		12:47-48 .	193, 196
	6:35 . . .	179		12:54-56 . .	246
	6:37,38,41-42 .	99		12:54-59 . .	80
	6:37-49 . .	156		12:57-59 .	138, 247
	6:39-40 . .	158		13:1-5, 6-9	247-248
				13:22-23 . .	239
				13:22-30 . .	171
				13:24 . . .	240

		Page Number				Page Number
Lk.	13:24-27 .	161-166	Lk.	17:28-30 .	.	251
	13:25 .	. 253		17:34-35 .	.	251
	13:26-27 .	240-242		17:37 .	.	251
	13:28-30 .	171, 241		18:1-8 .	181-186	
	13:31-33 .	. 245		18:9-14 .	199-201	
	13:34-35 .	224-225		19:11-28 .	192-195	
	14:28-35 .	. 258		19:26 .	.	195
	14:34-35 .	. 130		22:35-38 .	.	257
	16:1-13 .	. 155	Jn.	4:46-54 .	102, 170	
	16:1-9, 11-13	148-153,		6:14-15 .	.	210
		186-191,		6:22-65, 66-71	210	
		195		6:30 ff. .	151, 210	
	16:10 .	. 192		9:1-12 .	206-207	
	16:13 .	. 153		9:1-10:21	209, 211	
	16:14-15 .	. 197		9:40 ff. .	151, 159	
	16:14-31 .	. 155		13:16; 15:20	159	
	16:16-18 .	. 199		15-16 .	.	257
	16:17 .	. 133	Rom.	7:7 .	.	108
	16:18 .	89, 140	1 Cor.	1:24; 2:6-16 .	225	
	16:19-25 .	148, 200		9:9 .	.	46
	16:26-31 .	155, 200		13:3 .	.	14
	17:7-10 .	. 15	Gal.	6:1-4 .	.	156
	17:20-21 .	. 246	Jas.	1:25 .	.	7
	17:22-24, 25 .	. 252	2 Jn.	10-11 .	.	94
	17:26-27 .	. 250